KNOWLEDGE OF ACTION

SRI GARIB DASS ORIENTAL SERIES NO.—161

Knowledge of Action

Logico-Epistemological Analysis

R.I. INGALALLI

SRI SATGURU PUBLICATIONS
A Division of
INDIAN BOOKS CENTRE,
DELHI, INDIA

Published by :
SRI SATGURU PUBLICATIONS
Indological and Oriental Publishers
A Division of
INDIAN BOOKS CENTRE
40/5, Shakti Nagar,
Delhi-110007
(INDIA)

FIRST EDITION : DELHI, 1992

ISBN 81-7030-350-8.

Printed at :
Kiran Mudran Kendra
A-38/2 Maya Puri, Phase-I,
New Delhi-110064

PRINTED IN INDIA

CONTENTS

INTRODUCTION

In contemporary philosophy, analytical study of human action is considered to be an important aspect of philosophical inquiry in order to have a clearer understanding of human conduct. Clarification of 'human action' is extremely important not only for ethical purposes but also for relevant in every field of human life in which human beings constantly act and react together. In this book an attempt has been made to assess some of the recent views of analytical thinkers on voluntary action. I have also made an attempt to extract similar type of material from Indian sources mainly from Nyāya, Advaita and Mīmāṃsā systems in order to enrich our understanding of voluntary action. Attempts have been made to reconstruct some of the ideas on voluntary action. All the six chapters are interrelated as they consider the cluster of issues pertaining to action.

Chapter 1 : on voluntary action considers the problem of voluntary action as 'how are we to articulate necessary and sufficient conditions for voluntary action'. In order to find out a plausible answer to this question both positive and negative conditions of voluntary action have been examined with reference to the views of Danto (1973). Davidson (1985), Hempel (1965), Hudson (1970) and Searle (1984). After the assessment of their views, an attempt has been made to reconstruct an answer to the above question with reference to the theory of rigid designation. An adequate formulation regarding the nature of voluntary action consists of positive and negative conditions which also constitute necessary and sufficient conditions for a voluntary action as given below :

An act A is called voluntary if and only if

(i) n_1: an agent x performed it under no compulsion,

(ii) n_2: an agent x is not under ignorance,

(iii) n_3; an agent x is not surprised to do A,

(iv) p_1: an agent x intends to do A.

(v) p_2: an agent x successfully executes his intention to do A.

In the Second Chapter an attempt has been made to reconstruct a theory of explanation concerning human action. It is argued that Hempel's deductive nomological explanation and Davidson's causal explanation for voluntary action involve certain inadequacies. Normally rational actions are goal directed or value oriented. Since human beings are not just physical or mindless biological entities, their nature is constantly influenced by and modified by his culture. Human beings make plans and their actions are determined by a goal they seek to achieve. A behavioural criterion of purposive activity implies persistence and sensitivity toward the goal under varying conditions.

The Third Chapter explicates the structure of action sentences. Since action sentences are about human actions, formalisation of action sentences used in conversational language gives rise to considerable clarification of the notion of human action. In this regard it is argued that analysis of action sentences cannot be extended to non-action sentences. And following argument is shown to be valid :

1. A space-ship flight by me took place to Morning Star.
2. Morning Star=Evening Star.
3. A space-ship ∴ flight by me took place to Evening Star.

The rule of identity permits to draw (3 from (1) and (2).

Since action sentence is constituted by action terms, logical analysis of action term is important. An action term refers to an action. An action term is either a verb or a verbal noun. Action terms function like rigid designators. Action term may be singular or general. In either case they imply definite descriptions. If definite descriptions are unique then they imply unique properties about actions, consequently individuation of actions is feasible.

In the Fourth Chapter knowledge of voluntary action in

Navya-Nyāya is considered. The concept of kṛti as voluntary action plays a cardinal role in Navya-Nyāya, for it is presupposed in ethical discourses. In the course of the explicating the notion of kṛti necessary and sufficient conditions are considered. According to Viśvanātha an act a is voluntary if and only if (1) an agent desires to do a, (ii) he knows the feasibility of an act a through his effort, (iii) he has also knowledge of conduciveness of an act *a* and (iv) he also possesses knowledge of the means for doing *a*. In the process of analysis Prabhakara's objections are considered and assessed. Further the necessary and sufficient conditions of kṛti are compared with the conditions of voluntary action in Western context. It is shown that knowledge of kṛti implies knowledge of action in propositional sense of *knowing that* and non-propositional sense of *knowing how* to do an act ; actions are also knowable like other objects in the world.

In the Fifth Chapter of meaning of action sentences, an attempt has been made analyse the semantic status of action sentences in Indian and Western contexts. Is meaning of an action sentence an action, result of action or an agent of action ? According to Mīm̄ṃsakas activity is the meaning of action sentence. A transitive verb like 'to cook' implies the activity of an agent. Action sentences are closely related to imperatives because of imperatives are prior to events of actions that is to say that imperative causes a person to perform an act. On listening an imperative a person persues the goal i.e. to say that injunction is based upon the knowledge of causal relations holding between an act and the goal of agent. Normally an imperative expresses sābda-bhāvana and ārtha-bhāvana, Ārtha-bhāvana is the activity of an agent which causes something come into being it is the process denoted by the verb. And śābda bhāvana is that process which belongs to a word on its constituent element which induces an agent to undertake a course of action. In this context modern analysis of prescriptive sentence is considered. An ordinary imperative sentence lik (i) 'shut the door' is related to an ordinary factual judgment like (ii) 'you are going to shut the door'. However the two sentences are different because (i) is neither true nor false but (ii) must be either true or false depending upon the corresponding state of affair. On referential theory of meaning evaluative or imperative notion like 'ought' may not be considered as referring expression. However causal theory of meaning seems to be promising but even this theory has certain deficiency, for it does not make the distinction between the logical aspect of language and its psychological aspect relating dispositions occurring in hearer or speaker. Indian thinkers accommodate action language in their frame-work of language on the basis of logico-grammatical rules derived from the grammatical system of Pāṇini.

In the Sixth Chapter the notion of karma as voluntary action in Advaita system is considered. The notion of Karma plays an important role as an aid to jñāna-mārga. In his Bhagavadgīta-bhāṣya, Śri Śaṅkara acknowledges the purport of the verse 16 of Chapter IV by saying that even the wise men are deluded in respect of the question what karma (action) is and akarma (non-action) is. Even though every body is familiar with the action, it is not the case that action means exertion or movement of the body and inaction means to sit quiet. Śri Śaṅkara explicates the notions of action and inaction by defining the word 'action' as which is done. (karmani krīyate iti vyāpara mātram.) Both action and inaction presuppose an agent. There seems to be contradiction in saying that action is in ination and inaction in action. According to Śaṅkara there is no contradiction because from the point of view of an ignorant man what in reality is inaction appears as action and what in reality is action appears to be inaction, they are wrongly perceived. In this context we find an interesting theory of perception about acts or events. Both veridical and non-veridical perceptions are possible regarding human acts. That is to say action may be apprehended wrongly or rightly. Śri Śaṅkara gives an interesting analogy that no inaction is contained in action as jujube fruits (badari) are contained in a bawl; nor can action be said to be located in inaction for inaction is the absence of action. Only an ignorant man is likely to mistake action for inaction and conversely just as he mistakes water in mirage or silver in a conch shell.

The wise man or one who has realized the truth performs actions free from desires and purposes and in worldly life he becomes a best model for others. A wise man performs actions from spiritual point of view, he performs actions more efficiently than an ignorant man.

Normally actions are classified into satvic, rajasic and tamasic actions. A satvic action is free from attachment without love or hatred. An action is rajasic if it is done by one longing for pleasutes, such actions are done with egoistic mind. On the contrary an action performed by an ignorant person is tamasic for it is performed under delusion. The perfection in karma-yoga consists in bying qualified for jñāna-niśhṭhā. The state of freedom from action is attained by person whose mind is completely detached from the consequences of action except sattva-suddhi. An agent must have a concern with action alone but never with the fruits of action nor there should be any attachment for inaction. A karma is an intentional action (or voluntary action) because a karma is not blindly performed by the agents whether they are wise or ignorant. karma as an intentional action consists of agent's willing in one way or the other. It is possible to perform a given action with different intentions, An ordinary man performs un act *a* with an intention to enjoy its fruits but the same act *a* would be performed by spiritually inclined man (jñāni) for the sake of purification of internal organ (satva-śuddhi). 'karma' in its narrower sense stands for ritualistic karmas, in most general sense 'karma' designates action in general. Śaṅkāra did not advocate cessation of all activities in general, he encauroges actions conducive to self-realization. In this context certain similarities between Advaita criterion of moral action and Kant's categorical imperative are brought out. Kant's criterion of morality seems to be closure to the theory of niskāma-karma. It might be objected that if Brahman alone exists and the world of plurality is a shadow then there is no real distinction between right act and wrong act. This world is not mere illusion there is practical reality in it. Consequently for all practical purposes the world is real and moral values are valid as they lead to the supreme end. In the world love, wisdom and asceticism help to attain higher spiritual goals. There is the meaning for struggle with imperfection in order to realize the spiritual goal of self-realization.

1

ON VOLUNTARY ACTION

In this paper, I propose to examine positive and negative condions of voluntary action[1] with reference to the views of mainly, Danto (1973), Davidson (1985), Hempel, (1965), Hudson (1970), and Searle (1984). And in this regard I wish to formulate the problem of voluntary action as : How are we to articulate necessary and sufficient conditions for voluntary action ? In order to find out some plausible answer to this question, I would like to consider in the sequel the analysis of negative and positive conditions of voluntary action. After the assessment of the views on negative and positive conditions, I make an attempt to reconstruct my answer to the above question with reference to the theory of rigid designation.

An inquiry into the notion of voluntary action (rational action) ought to begin with the idea of rationality[2] which plays an important role ; I have to consider some remarks on the notion of rationality On Brandt's view (198 : 125-30) practical rationality is concerned with choices that would survive criticism. Normally a given action is qualified as ration action (i.e. voluntary action) by way of putting forward an empirical hypothesis and acritical appraisal (Hempel 1965 : 463). On Hempel's view the hypothes is is about the action which was done for certain reasons so that it can be explained in terms of motivating reasons. And the reasons usually include the ends that the agent sought to and beliefs concerning the availability, propriety and possible means of attaining them. The critical appraisal is characterised by the course of action involving a reasonable or appropriate choice of means for achieving certain end Hempel (464) thinks that : "If we are to choose a rational course of action in pursuit of given ends, we will have to take into account all available information concerning such matters as the particular circumstances in which the action is to be taken; different means by which, in these circumstances, the given ends might be attained; and the side-effects and after effects that may be expected from the use of different available means." Hempel seems to imply that certain mode of choosing an action considered to be rational course of action, i.e. to say that intention is required for execution of an action. However agent's intention need not yield an action. Thus it is desirable to inquire into the necessary and sufficient conditions of voluntary action (rational action).[3]

In order to seek an answer to the question what conditions, negative and positive must be fulfilled if the action is to be considered as a voluntary action (i.e. rational action), authors like Hudson (1970 : 335-38) prefer to consider two negative conditions originally conceived by Aristotle (Nichomachean Ethics III) namely n1 : absence of external compulsion, and n2 : absence of agent's[4] ignorance. I wish to add n3 : i.e. absence of surprise in an agent (a condition suggested by Wittgenstein[5]). Regarding n1, Hudson (335) thinks : action will be voluntary if and only if it is not due to external compulsion. This formulation seems to be defective due to his usage of 'iff' which is normally used to qualify a certain condition as a sufficient condition. However, if n1 is a necessary condition, it cannot be a sufficient condition for rational action, and for the same reason it will not do for n2 as Hudson (335) says "... an action is voluntary... if and only if it is not due to agent's ignorance". However it is necessary to look closely into the conditions n1 and n2. For clearer understanding of n1 and n 2 we have to refer to Aristotle's views on voluntary and involuntary actions. According to Aristotle[6] a man who acts voluntarily originates such action within himself i.e. the individual is the locus of action and consequently he is called the agent of voluntary actions. And in contradistinction with voluntary action there is an involuntary action caused by external circumstances and there is no agent's contribution for that act. Hudson (335) illustrates n1 by saying that while some one driving his car, if he were pushed in the back by one of his passengers; he moved his car on a wrong side. In this case driving a car on wrong side is not a deliberate or voluntary action, because it happened due to external compulsion. But what constitutes an external compulsion ? If some one is allowed by a dictator to choose between either obeying or disobeying him, then there is a choice f r acting one way or the other. Since every action performed under compulsion is an involuntary action and if a particular action is performed due to choice under compulsion, then that act is also involuntary act.

By definition involuntary action lacks intention. And on the contrary, action performed in the absence of external compulsion is normally conceived in some way to originate in the choice, intention, or will of an agent.[7] In case of n2 i.e. absence of agent's ignorance, there seems to be the satisfaction of the condition nl (also) in order that an agent could perform his intended act. If the driver moved his vehicle to the wrong side due to his ignorance about faulty brakes then that is not considered to be a voluntary action. Once again as in the case of absence of nl, in case of absence of n2 there is absence of appropriate intention corresponding to the given act. Because, had the driver been aware of faulty breakes he would not have driven the vehicle on the wrong side. However an action peɩformed under ignorance need not be the action performed under external compulsion. Regarding the relationship between nl and n2 following points hold good. An act performed under n 1 (i.e. absence of external compulsion) need not imply that the given act satisfies n2 (i.e. the absence of ignorance). And conversely, an act performed in the absence of ignorance need not imply the absence of external compulsion. In the absence of external compulsion an agent is likely to act ignorantly, hence the necessity of n2 i.e. absence of ignorance; and n2 implies the positive condition of awareness or agent's knowledge.

Now let me consider n3: the absence of surprise. According to Wittgenstein (1953 : 162), voluntary movement (action) is marked by the absence of surprise. Let us consider Wittgenstein's description of voluntary action. He says : "I form the decision to pull the bell at 50 'clock, and when it strikes 5, my arm makes this movement. Is that the correct description and not this one :. . . and when it strikes 5' raise my arm ?"... I do not say 'see my arm is going up' when I raise it. So one might say : Voluntary movement is marked by the absence of surprise". Wittgenstein implies that the absence of surprise is just a necessary condition but not sufficient condition. To this effect Prof. Strawson[8] (1974 : 162) observes : "As a sufficient condition this (absence of surprise) will not do". He seems to imply that absence of surprise functions as one of the necessary conditions for voluntary act. Surely Wittgenstein does not qualify absence of surprise as sufficient condition of voluntary action because he also considers other (necessary) conditions required for voluntary action. For instance formation of intention or volition prior to execution of an act is also a necessary condition for voluntary act.

The absence of surprise (n3) and absence of ignorance (n2) are interrelated. Normally ignorance implies surprise; so absence of surprise implies absence of ignorance. To the above (n 1 and n2) negative conditions Hudson (338) adds some more conditions like absence of compulsive psychological mechanisms like kleptomania and absence of dispositions like nervousness, cowardice, however such conditions may be included under n2 i.e. absence of ignorance, because if an agent is aware of his limitations, he is likely to change his course of action by adopting suitable means to overcome those limitations. Or even he may take a decision to abstain from performing the act until favourable conditions occur.

Positive conditions of voluntary action. Normally intention of an act prior to the performance of the act is considered to be a positive condition.[8] Since intention of an agent implies agent's free choice in doing a certain act; it is necessary to analyse the locution "of the agent's own choice". On Hudson's (338) view "action is voluntary, if and only if it is done of the agent's own choice". But this formulation is defective because the phrase 'agent's own choice' does not function as sufficient condition but it is to be qualified as a necessary condition only. Even if we consider agent's own choice as a necessary condition of voluntary action, the question arises namely how is agent's choosing to X related to his doing X ? Various attempts have been made to tackle this question. On Moore's view[9] "I can do X" should be analysed as "I can do X, if I choose 'X' or I shall do X, if I choose 'X'. Moore says : "Many of our actions are under the control of our will, in the sense that if, just before we began to do them, we had chosen not do them, we *should* not have done them, and I propose to care call all actions of this kind *votuntary actions*[10]. But from such a view on voluntary action it is difficult to make out the exact significance of 'I can do X if I choose X' because Moore prefers to give a negative version of voluntary action to explain a positive condition of agent's own choice. What is the significance of "if" in the above sentence ? Moore intended it to be an "if" of a causal condition because he wanted to give an intepretation of voluntary action in terms of causation.[11] On Hudson's view "I can do X, if I choose" is not a sufficient condition because agent's choice or decision to do an action is itself insufficient to cause the action. And there must be other conditions like agent's ability, and opportunity to do the action must be fulfilled. Austin[12] reacts to Moore's view (mentioned above) by contending that "the things we ordinarily say about what we can do or could have done" show that the "if" in "I can if I choose" is not or not always, the "if" of the condition but rather the "if" of doubt or hesitation. On Austin's view "if" does not indicate a causal link and hence there is no adequate contra-position corresponding to 'I can do X, if I choose X'. In case of 'If p then q' where the 'if' stands for sufficient condition, then the contra-positive 'If not q then not p' can be inferred. Now consider the contra-positive of "I could have done X, which I did not do, if "I had chosen" as "If I could not have done X, which I did not do, then I had not chosen". According to Austin it does not make any sense because "If" lacks the force of conditionality. However Hudson does not see any absurdity or oddity in forming the above contra-position, for he prefers to see a necessary condition in a statement instead of sufficient condition. To this effect authors like O' Connor,[13] think that statements of the form "If p then q" often state a necessary condition, consequently it is not odd to say "If we take the nine fifty-five (train), we shall be in London by one o'clock". In this example taking the nine fifty-five (train) is not the sufficient condition but only one of the necessary conditions of our reaching London. Similarly one may consider "I could have done X, which I did not do, if I had chosen" as a statement of necessary condition is equivalent (in meaning) to 'I could not have done X, which I, did not do, if I had not chosen' (If not p then not q). Since contra-positive form of 'If not p then not q' is 'If q then p', the corresponding contra-positive statement for the above statement is : 'If I could have done X, which I did not do, then I had chosen.[14]

Even though such a proposal seems to be intelligible, there are difficulties. One of the difficulties in this context I would like to point out is that from a logical point of view statements involving modal auxiliaries like 'could' used above are truth functionally opaque and law of contra-position hardly works in such cases. And for adequate analysis of such statements it is desirable to apply the techniques of modal logic. However in case of contra-position, a necessary condition means one's ability to do X as conditional upon one's 'choosing to do it. However the implication of 'could have done X, which I did not do if I had chosen' is that some one had the ability to do it, even though he did not choose to exercise this ability. Of course 'if' clause stating a necessary condition may not cause a difficulty in understanding the difference between 'choosing to do X' and 'doing X'. But Hudson (344) argues that often we do not have adequate empirical grounds for affirming that there are two occurrences when an agent does some thing which he can do. And some times agents are also not aware of having first chosen to do an act and then having done it. Secondly, keeping of the difference between an act and the act of choosing to do it as a pre-condition leads to an infinite regress because act of choosing is itself doing something which the agent can do but in that case also there are two occurrences : Choosing to choose to do and choosing to do and so on. I wish to meet the above objection by way of referring to one of the negative conditions of voluntary action namely absence of ignorance. Presence of ignorance in human action qualifies that action is involuntary or irrational action. However regarding the second objection, one might say there is no chance for infinite regress if an individual is free to choose but not conditioned in choosing. Since in the above analysis of 'I can do X, if I choose to do X' as a positive condition is not actually the analysis of an action done by the agent but it provides as understanding of prior intention for voluntary action.

Since intention as a positive condition (pl) constitutes an

important aspect of voluntary action, it is necessary to explicate the notion of intention.[15] Normally a certain intention is satisfied if the corresponding action represented by the content of the intention is actually performed. For example 'Smith intends to vote for Jones' is carried out if he votes for Jones. Intention as a necessary condition of voluntary action normally formed prior to actions, because of his desire as also of his awareness of consequences. The usual form of expression of a prior intention "I will do A" or "I am going to do A" is to be distinguished from an intention in action "I am doing A". To this effect Searle (1984:84) says: "We say of a prior intention that the agent acts on his intention, or that he carries out his intention, or that he tries to carry it out; but in general we can't say such things of intentions in actions, because the intention in action just is the intentional content of the action; the action and the intention are inseparable." Searle implies that only intentional actions have intentional content or every voluntary action has intentional content. He prefers to distinguish between an intention in action and prior intention. Many actions are performed without previous intention. For example some one gets up and starts pacing about the room and such actions are considered to be intentional without forming prior intention. Consequently every intentional action has intention in action but an intentional action need not have prior intention.

We find some difference between the views of Searle and Davidson. On Davidson's view intentions normally cause actions, for instance prior intention to raise an arm causes the act of raising that arm. However Searle thinks that one might perform the action of raising one's arm in a way that had nothing to do with his prior intention. His reason is that a person might forget all about his intention and later raise his arm for some other reason. But even in that case there is intention because it is not a question of what sort of intention is needed to raise the arm but there must be some intention either of one type or the other which is prior to the act of raising one's arm. In other words corresponding to a given act of raising one's arm there may be different intentions. For example Smith raised his arm because he intended to greet his friend; however he might have raised his arm for some other intention say to stop his friend.

There is also Wittgenstein's (1953:161e) problem of intention: When I raise my arm, my arm goes up. And the problem arises: What is left over if I subract the fact that my arm goes up from the fact that I raise my arm?" His answer is kinaesthetic experience and willing.[16] However authors like Searle (1984:16) try to interpret Wittgenstein's answer by saying that what is left is an intentional content that my arm goes up as a result of this intention in action. Searle (87) thinks that Wittgenstein's question is some what analogous to the question: If I see the table what is left over if I substract the table? And the answer is that a certain form of presentational intentionality is left over, i.e. to say that what is left over in the case of a visual perception is a visual experience. Similarly in the case of action what is left over is an experience of acting and the arm raising experience has an intentional content. If the arm goes up without intention then the arm is not raised but it just went up. Thus an act of raising the arm implies the intention to raise that arm.

However authors like Strawson (1974:161) react to Wittgenstein's problem in a slightly different way. Strawson reformulates the problem as : "How do you know that you have raised your arm (if the eyes are shut)? The answer that 'I feel it', may not be satisfactory because there may not be invariable conomitance between the special feeling (kinesthetic sensation) and the raising of the arm. However the certainty that you have raised your arm is itself a criterion or recognising the feeling here. Strawson seems to imply that an act backed up by intention or feeling serves as a criterion of intention or feeling. But there is also the question of the criterion of voluntary action, which seems to be more relevant for the present purpose of explicating the notion of intention as a necessary condition of voluntary action.

If there is a distinction between prior intentions and intentions in action, there is a need to understand the interrelationship among prior intention, intention in action, awareness of bodily movement, and an actual act. An act of raising one's arm, contains two components namely, the experience of acting and the event of one's arm going up. Normally the intentional content of the intention in action is the same as the experience of acting because the experience of acting is a conscious experience with an intentional content. Searle (92) may not be right in saying that sometimes one performs intentional actions without any conscious experience of doing so, one of the necessary conditions of intentional action is intention characterised by an element of awareness regarding agent's act. A voluntary act like 'X raised his arm' is to be analysed as follows :

(i) X had a prior intention to raise, at t1, his arm, and

(ii) acting on that intention, X raises his arm at t2.

(iii) X's arm goes up as a result of intention in action.

In such contexts authors like Davidson,[17] Searle (94) and others bring in the notion of causation. Searle for example, thinks that the prior intention causes both the intention in action and bodily movement as shown in the following diagram :

causes causes
prior intention— — —intention in action — — — bodily movement.
←— ——— —action— — — ———— —— - —→

Here causal element is indispensable and such a model gives rise ta certain difficulties also. Firstly prior intention is only a necessary condition but not a sufficient one for voluntary action. Secondly even if intentions cause actions in the way described above it is not correct to explain an action by referring i's intention. Because to the 'question' why did X raise his arm? it would be odd to say, 'because he intended to raise his arm'. An appropriate answer would be: He was exercising; waving goodbye etc. Authors like Ayer (19`6:3-4) are skeptical about causal explanation for human action, even if human actions as physical movements have their mental antecedents. According to Davidson, (1985:1-19) mental events under mental descriptions are subject to strict causal laws. However on Ayer's view it is not possible to pin-point the mental events for mental descriptions and there may not be sufficient information from subject's behaviour to be sure about the accuracy of mental descriptions; and there is no proof for causal determination or non-causal explanation of an act. However for understanding the notion of intention as a necessary positive) condition for voluntary action reference to causal model or non-causal model is of secondary importance. Because a necessary condition may be a causal condition or an element of reason in the form of some antecedent factor.

A prior intention may be analysed in terms of beliefs and desires. If X has prior intention to perform A, he must believe that it is possible to do A and X must have desire to do A. In other words intention is structured in appropriate beliefs and desires. There is some intentional state S for X such that S contains: X's belief in the possibility of doing A and X's desire to do A and X's belief that S will function causally toward production : X will do A and X's desire that S will cause A so that X will do A. Searle's (104) reason for not accepting the above analysis of intention is that even after the fulfilment of above conditions, X might not form an intention to do A. Searle seems to add an additional condition to the above list to give a complete characterisation of intention. Even if there is an additional condition required for an intention' it is not possible to consider intention itself as a sufficient condition for voluntary action because intentions alone do not bring appropriate action. It is necessary to find out some other additional positive condition required for voluntary action.

Whenever an agent tries to perform an intentional act satisfying the above mentioned conditions both positive and negative hemay or may not actualize or realize his action by way of carrying out the corresponding intention. If he successfully executes (carries) out his intention along with other necessary conditions there is the realization of the act. Thus successful execution is second positive condition (p2) of voluntary action. Execution normally implies the fulfilment of agent's intention to do some thing.

Now I wish to give a consolidated formulation regarding the nature of voluntary action in terms of negative and posive conditions which, perhaps, constitute necessary and sufficient conitions for a voluntary action.

An act A is called voluntary act if and only if

(i) (n1) : an agent X performed it under no compulsion,

(ii) (n2) : an agent X is not under ignorance,

(iii) (n3) : an agent X is not surprised to do A,

(iv) (p1) : an agent X intends to do A,

(v) (p2) : an agent X successfully executes his intention to do A.

I think above characterisation of voluntary action covers both basic and non-basic types of voluntary actions. Since non-basic action is constituted by basic action, it is necessary to consider the notion of basic action Danto (1973 : 7) uses the expression 'mDa' as convenient short hand for 'm makes happen the event *a* by doing a'. D makes the assertion that *a* was done or *a* is an event properly called as an action, so that following analysis holds good : m intends that *a* happen, a happens, m does *b* and *b* is adequate for *a*. Of course this analysis fits for a non-basic action, because there is an event distinct from *a*, *b* is done by m and that *a* happens since *b*, happens Here the question is to determine what sort of context i· required for *b* if it is to be a basic action. Often it is difficult to determine whether a description is basic or non-basic; 'm D a' may be a basic description or a non-basic description. In describing *b* as a basic action one has to provide a basic description of *b* in which an agent directly caused it to happen. And basic actions have no components; m immediately causes *b* is illustrated in the following way. Let (e)—the throwing of the stone causes m to raise his arm *b* (but does not cause rising of the arm itself) and the raising arm is caused by the flexing of a triceps (f) and m immediately causes (b) because 'mDf' is not a component of m Db (Danto : 59). This is rather puzzling because mDb itself is a consequence of m Df. Searle and Davidson react differently to Danto's notion of basic action. Searle (100) defines basic action as follows :

"A is a basic action type for an agent S if S, is able to perform acts of type A and S can intend to do an act of type A without intending to do any other action by means of which he intends to do A". Searle implies that corresponding to given basic action A there is unique intention say X which is not an intention for some other action B. However there is an open question that is basic action characterised by basic intention ? Neither Danto nor Searle postulate the notion of basic intention. However on Searle's view above definition of basic action is relative to an agent and his skills, so that what is basic for one agent might be non-basic for another. For example, for a good skier basic action is involved in his making a left turn based on his intention to do so. However for a beginner an act of making a left turn is non-basic or complex act because in order to make a left turn he has to put his weight on the down hill ski, while edging it into the slope, then shift the weight from left to right ski etc , and such sequences may be called content of his intentions in action. Thus for Searle there is no sharp line of distinction between basic and non-basic actions.

Davidson (56-7) reacts differently by saying there is a confusion in Danto's distinction between basic acts such as moving a hand and other acts that are caused by the basic acts such as moving a stone. Davidson points out a mistake in thinking that when some one closes the door, the action of moving hand causes the closing of the door. Or it is wrong to say that action of closing the door is caused by moving the hand. Davidson implies that there is no causal relation among acts or one type of act need not lead to another type of act.

However the notion of basic act seems to be indispensable in performing complex acts because normally the attainment of ability in performing a complex act is due to efficient performances of unit acts constituting a complex act. A given complex act need not be caused by the elements of that act. In a complex act like typing there are unit acts which are simple and basic to the complex act of typing. An act of pressing a single key at a time is a simple or basic act and the sequence of many such acts constitute the complex act of typing in general.

Normally action terms designate actions the manner in which general names or proper names refer to their referents. An action term is derived from the corresponding verb, and such term are called verbal nouns or gerunds, which in turn are called as action terms. 'Typing' is, formed from the verb 'to type', 'printing' from 'to print' and so on. In this context I would like to consider the question: Are action terms rigid designators? In the usual standard literature on rigid designation we normally do not find the explication of action terms as rigid designators. In order to consider them as rigid designators I get some indirect clue from Salmon's[18] (1982:42) view that the theory of rigid designation may even be extended to verbs. Putnam[19] (1975) thinks of extension of the theory of rigid designation to natural kind verbs such as 'grow'. If every name is rigid designator and action terms are also names, then action terms are also rigid designators. But what is a rigid designator? On Kripke's[20] formulation, 'a term is a rigid designator if and only if it designates the same referent in every possible world if it exists'. Accordingly an action term (t) is a rigid designator if and only if it refers to the same act (a) in every possible world if that act occurs. For example an action term like 'typing' is a rigid designator if and only if it refers to the act of typing in every possible state of affair if that act is present. Thus an act is a bearer of rigid designator. But this claim is to be examined. An important feature of rigid decsignator is that it is non-descriptional. That is to say that descriptions pertaining to accidental properties of referents are world bound because such definite descriptions hold good in some possible worlds but not in every possible world. However a definite description pertaining to essential property is considered to be a rigid designator. For example the definite description 'the element with atomic number 79' rigidly designates Gold only. However in case of 'Gold is yellow metal', the predicate 'yellow metal' does not rigidly designate the same matter gold in every possible world if it exists because 'being yellow' is only contingent property and pure gold is normally white in colour. Similarly if action term is a rigid designator then that term is non-descriptional with reference to contingent descriptions of a given act. If an action term (t) rigidly designates an act (a) (i.e. human act) then 't' is non-descriptional across the possible worlds. And the action term (t) is conferential with the description of unique or essential nature of that act so that a proposition containing action term (t) and definite description (dd) pertaining to essential nature of the act is qualified as a necessary a posteriori statement. Because 't' and 'dd' are rigid designators and if the sentence is true then it is necessary truth and a posteriori nature of such sentence is due to the empirical discovery. To some extent this mode of understanding may be extended (to the domain of human actions also. There are many human actions, which may be called as natural (voluntary) actions namely 'walking', 'eating', 'drinking' etc. and there are artificial human acts such as 'travelling', 'driving', 'typing: etc. An act is capable of being desc ibed both in terms of indefinite descriptions and definite descriptions. And both the types of descriptions of an act normally emerge from agent's knowing how to do a certain act. For instance an act of typing is described as that human act in which pressing of keys in quick succession occurs, pressing of keys is to be done in accordance with certain laws, plus other allied movements like handling a mob and turning a wheel etc. However it may not be the case that where there is the operation of the keys involving pressing the keys in quick succession is an act of typing. Because there may be other acts like operating a computer where one may find similar acts. However an act in order to be qualified as an act of typing must satisfy some unique characteristic in virtue of which it is called as an act of typing. Consequently every human act is unique in the sense that with reference to unique property of an act it is possible individuate or identify a given act. Given an act 'a' and p1, p2, etc. (pn) are descriptions of a, following normally hold good.

(i) 'a=p1+p2+**pn'.

(ii) 'a is p1' if true and p1, 'non-rid designator then (ii) is contingently true.

(iii) 'a is p2' if true and 'a' and 'p2' are rigid designator then then (iii) is necessary proposition and

(iv) 'a is pn' if true and 'a' and 'pn' are ridid designators then (iv) is necessarily true.

Consider the sentence 'Devadatta cooks'. In this sentence the transitive verb 'cook' implies the act of 'cooking'. And the act of cooking itself described in terms of series of functions performed in a proper sequence observing the rules of cooking etc, Even though it is possible to give traditional and modern descriptions of cooking, apart from certain differences in two methods of cooking, the act of cooking is basically same with reference to its unique functlon. Similarly an act of driving a car is same whether it was performed in case of one type of vehicle (car) or another. In other words different tokens of acts are same as the corresponding type of act. However the theory of rigid designation as the theory of direct reference is subject io criticisms. Authors like Linsky (1977:42-4) try to repudiate the non-descriptional view of rigid designators by saying that the role of definite descriptions is crucial in fixing the reference of a term. Without pursuing a critical inquiry in this regard I would like to make the following observations on rigid designators with reference to action terms. The action terms are relatively rigid designators because they are the names of acts, and prior to naming of an act name may not designate any thing. And act or things as bearers o? name can exist without names. However names are convenient conceptual devices to understand the facts in the world. Whenever action terms designate some actions, they also imply important features of those acts. Consequently they may be called descriptional in nature, and even the theory of direct reference itself allows definite descriptions of unique properties as rigid designators,

In case of voluntary action considered above the set of necessary and sufficient conditions fix up the reference of action term. And the fixation of reference of action term pertaining to voluntary action qualifies that action terms as relatively rigid designator. That is to say that an action term refers to voluhtary action if and only if the term is descriptional in terms of necessary and sufficient conditions of voluntary action.[20]

NOTES

1. Human actions in general may be classified into voluntary actions and involuntary actions. Normally involuntary actions are un-intentional actions. But see Searle (1984:101-2). Davidson (1985:4-5) thinks that actions, performances and events not involving intentions are alike. However Davidson's (5) position is paradoxical because he says that even though the word 'action' does not very often occur in ordinary speech he prefers

to use the word 'action' for anything an agent does intentionally, including intentional Comissions. He considers 'A' is description of an action, 'B' is a description of some thing done voluntarily, though un-intentionally and 'C' is a description of something done involuntarily and unintentionally. However he cannot make a supposition that A-B-C in order to consider the question about the sameness of A, B and C. Because action is normally what is done by an agent and an event is that which just occurs. Consequently an action of 'raising one's arm' cannot be identical with a bodily movement of 'One's arm going up',

2. The idea of rationality plays a crucial role in explicating the notion of voluntary action. Because it has double function, firstly voluntary action is structured in agent's reason in terms of which agent is said to be responsible for his action. Secondly rationality as a criterion of voluntary action provides a frame work for accounting such acts in terms of general laws so that they are adequately explained. And in this direction authors like Hempel consider the possibility of providing (rational) explanation on the basis of deductive nomological scheme. Of course Davidson (1985:265) differs from Hempel in this regard.

3. Some current theories of voluntary action by Prichard, Davidson and Sellars are considered to be rival theories (Aune-1977:1-46). Accorping to Prichared an action must be understood as the process or activity of willing itself and in the process physical movement as a result cannot be considered to be as caused by willing. Thus action as an activity is not to be identified as some-thing originating in some other thing. Davidson (1985:3-19) argues for the causal theory of action. However assessment of the rival theories of involuntary action is not intended here. An inquiry into necessary and sufficient conditions of voluntary action seems to be relevant for any theory of voluntary action.

4. While understanding the notion of agency, Davidson (1985;43-61) considers the relation between an agent and action. See Aristotle (1949:110a), Aune (1977:11-12); Danto (1973:55,119).

5. Wittgenstein (1953;162); see Strawson (1974:162).

6. Aristotle (1944:1109^{b}) makes the distinction between voluntary action and involuntary action with reference to an agent

to the former. Accordingly any action done or performed by an agent need not be voluntary action unless it is grounded in agent's own choice and intention.

7. Hudson (1970;334); Aristotle (1949:1110[a], 1109[b]).

8. Anscombe (1976:1-5), Aune (1977:8-12), Danto (1973:79-100 : Davidson (1985:1-19), Hudson (1970:338); Searle (1984:79-100); Quinn (1989:294).

9. Moore (1959:10-11) seems to consider species of voluntary acts relevant in moral discourse. And a moral discourse which normally presupposes a human act is a voluntary act and such act is subject to moral evaluation so that the act under consideration is either right or wrong. There are alternative theories of moral evaluation. Moore's ethical theory is generally called as ethical intuitionism. See Hudson (1970:339); Austin (1961:153-80).

10. Quoted by Hudson (1970-340).

11. Austin (1961:159); Hudson (1970:340).

12. Austin (1961:153) considers the question: Are cans constitutionally if's ? And then he goes on sorting out different uses of 'if' and points out that if as a conditional does not fit in Moore's view: 'I can do X if I choose X'.

13. Hudson (1930;342).

14. Let me consider Davidson's (66-7) reactions to Moore and Austin. He considers Moore's formulation that 'A can do X' means 'If A chooses to do X then he does X'. For exampl(, 'Jones can anchor his boat in the channel' means 'If Jones chooses to anchor his boat in the – channel'. Davidson tries to examine Austin's attack on Moore with reference to his proposal, On Davidson's view Moore sees no important difference between 'A does X if he chooses and 'A can do X if he chooses'. And Austin's argument is faulty because he (Austin) assumes that if A does X if he chooses' means, the same as 'A can do X if he chooses', then 'does' and 'can do' must mean the same. This is wrong because 'does' and 'can do' donot mean the same and yet the sentences 'A does X if he chooses' and 'A can do X if he chooses' are equivalent, granted that 'A can do X' means 'A does X if he chooses'. Even though Austin is right in saying that 'A can do X if he chooses to do X' is not a causal or conditional, it

In the theory of decision making various models of rational choice have been constituted as utilities of different total outcomes.

In this context it would be an interesting point to consider Hempel's (469) criticism of Dray's concept of rational explanation. On Dray's view explanation by motivating reasons displays the rational of what was done. Rational explanation is offered in terms of "a reconstruction of the agent's calculation of means to be adopted toward his chosen end in the light of the circumstances in which he found himself. To explain the action we need to know what considerations convinced him that he should act as he did".[3] Dray also attributes *evaluative* concept to rational explanation. Accordingly the agent had good reasons for his action (as rational/explanation) must invoke a "*principle of action*" which is not an empirical law. The principle of action expresses a judgment of the form : When in a situation of type C_1... Cn the thing to do is X (cited in Hempel 470), this principle contains an element of appraisal of what was done, Dray sees the fundamental difference between rational explanations of natural phenomenon by subsuming it under covering general law and rational explanation involving an element of appraisal in the context of rational or voluntary actions. Hempel thinks that Dray does not specify some relevant factors such as the end the agent sought to attain, agent's beliefs regarding the attainment of his objective and moral or religious norms committed by the agent. According to Dray the conception of rational explanation answers the question why did agent A do X ? by offering an explanans. Following is a schema S^1 reformulated by Hempel.

Explanans : { A was in a situation of type C.
In a situation of type C, the appropriate thing to do is X (normative principle of action).

Therefore, A did X (explanandum)

Hempel (470) thinks that this type of rational explanation will not do, for it presupposes a criterion of rationality for a particular course of action as the thing to do, and the information that agent A was in a situation of kind C but these are no grounds for believing that A did infact do X. There is a necessity of further explanatory assumption that A was a rational agent and was disposed to do X under the given circumstances. Hempel's gives the following argument having the schema (S'), as a satisfactory answer to the question why did A do X[4].

S2:	A was in a situation of type C.
	A was a rational agent.
Explanans	In a situation of type C, any rational agent will do X (Empirical principle of action).
	Therefore, A did X (Explanandum.)

The schema S2 differs from S1 in two respects : (i) S2 consists of the assumption that A was a rational agent (as a second premise of S2), and (ii) the evaluative principle of action is replaced by an empirical generalization stating how rational agents will perform action of a given kind in a situation of type C. Consequently S2 restores the covering-law form to explain human actions. Hempel implies that it would be irrelevant to argue that X was indeed 'the thing to do' but it would be relevant to show that A was generally disposed to do X under given conditions. However Hempel does not deny the view that an explanatory account overtones but he maintains that whether a critical appraisal is irrelevant to its explanatory force and an appraisal alone as a principle of action cannot explain why A did in fact do X. But what is the nature of a rational agent in S2 ? For Hempel it is a descriptive psychological notion and normative or evaluative connotations are inessential for its explanatory use because to say of someone that he is a rational agent is to attribute to him set of dispositions as tendencies to behave in particular way in the background of agent's objectives, beliefs his psychological and biological state. Consequently explanation of an action is to be given in terms of agent's reasons and general tendencies.

Hempel's covering law model of explanation has been refuted by writers like Davidson. It is necessary to consider Davidson's position regarding explanation of voluntary actions. Davidson identifies the role of causal concepts in the description and explanation of human action. He reacts against a view that the explanation of an intentional action in terms of its motives or reasons could not relate reasons and actions as cause and effect. He argues that even though causal relations are generally nomological based on induction while one understanding that an agent has acted on certain reasons is not dependent on indutcion or laws. Even though he acknowledges Hempel as an early partisan of the causal view of action, he takes issue with him on the role of empirical laws in explaining actions; he accepts the view that teleological explanation of action differs from explanation in the natural sciences on the ground that laws are not essential in the former. Davidson (1985:262) subscribes to the view that our understanding of actions leads to causal relation i.e to say that beliefs and desire cause actions; this view is also acceptable to Hempel. Davidson thinks that there is a weak sense in which a law may be involved, in case of A causes B such that descriptions of A and B fall under a law. However agent's reasons do not involve laws. Actions can be explained by reference to reasons without laws that link them. Davidson (263) doubts the applicability of covering-law-model to human acts, for it is possible to deduce explanandum from a false law in conjunction with relevant singular fact. He offers the following example. A certain individual, Ada performs an act of pressing in succession the seven, the two, the nine and the cube root buttons on her calculator in order to take the cube root of 729. Her reasoning or explanation for the act may be expressed in deductive-nomological schema S3 as :

(i) Any action of mine that is a taking of the cube root of 729 is desirable; (ii) my pressing in succession the seven, two, nine and cube root buttons will be such an action, (iii) So, my pressing those buttons is desirable. Davidson's (263) modified version of it is as follows S4:- Ada wants to take the cube root of 729. Ada's want is or entails a certain disposition to act to obtain what one wants. That some one has a certain disposition may be expressed as a generalization or law governing the behaviour of that person. In the present case, if Ada thinks some action will constitute her taking the cube root of 729, she will take that action She thinks that pressing the 7, 2, 9 and the cube root buttons in succession will constitute such an action. So, she presses the buttons. According to Davidson[5] the 'law' is false because often people do not perform the action to achieve a desired end though they possess certain relevant dispositions. However it is necessary to investigate

the causal theory. (i) Since primary reasons consists of attitudes and beliefs which are dispositions or states and they are not events, therefore they are not causes. (ii) A reason in order to be a cause must be logically distinct from the alleged effect but it is not so; therefore reasons are not causes. (iii) Normally human beings possess knowledge of reasons in acting without presupposing a causal relation between reasons and actions that is to say that a person knows his own intentions in acting without observation or induction. Thus causality is not indispensable in explaining human actions. Authors like Davidson try to reply to these arguments in order to establish the view that reasons are the causes of an act. Regarding (i) it is argued that mental states, dispositions and conditions are frequently named as the causes of events. Because mental states are also in the form of intention prior to an act. Further it is an action intelligible by redescribing it, hence under different descriptions causality works. The truth of a causal statement depends upon the description of events.

Reply to (iii) : Even though knowledge of intentions in acting is peculiar to first person knowledge of one's own beliefs, desires and so on, it does not imply that reasons do not cause actions And causal laws need not be law-like generalizations but they may be singular causal statements.

Above replies to the critique of causal theory of action are not very sound. There seems to be an ambiguity regarding the notion of cause (a) "cause in the usual sense implies a totality of conditions indispensable for an event (effect) to take place. In this sense both cause and effect have on the same ontological footing. (b) The word cause is also understood in a loose sense for anything that precedes any other event through invariable concomitance. Often the language of action seems to be the language of event. However if an act k was done of an agent's own choice, then there need not be a postulation of causal connection between the events-choosing to do k and doing x. Normally rational action is equated with causal view by treating reasons as causes will not do, for there is a logical distinction between cause and reason. If causal view of human action is not unsatisfactory, it is not possible to offer deductive-nomological explanation also. Rational actions and natural events are different, even though former also occur in the observable world. Rational actions are unlike natural events, they are guided by human volitions, desires etc. packed in intentions. Thus human actions need a kind of explanation in terms of individual's goals and available means for the successful performance of a given act, such type of explanation is teleological in nature. However Davidson's teleological explanation is extremely subjective and hence individualistic. It is necessary to workout objective type of teleological explanation for voluntary actions.

Reconstruction of explanation for voluntary action (rational action) in terms of objective teleological laws : In this reconstruction there are two parts : (A) in this part certain limitations of deductive-nomological explanations are considered in the proper perspective and in B) there is an attempt to reformulate the teleological sentences so that they adequately function as legitimate formulas in the explanans in order to explain the corresponding explanandum. A: In the covering law of explanation an important idea is that the occurrence of an event is explained if it is subsumed under a law of nature so that an event occurred in conformity with some general regularity of nature. Usual logical form of an explanation is as follows :

S1 ....Sn G1 ....Gn	The explanans

∴ E The explanandum

In this schema there are two sets of premises namely a set of singular statements S1..... Sn about relevant conditions and a set of general laws G1 .... Gn as covering laws. If the explanandum E is deduced from the explanans then E describes the phenomenon to be explained.[7] In this deductive model of explanation every explanation must invoke some general law of nature. And such explanation is also called a causal explanation because the premises give rise to an explanandum. A law like statement or law of universal forms affirms that every event of kind F is invariably followed an event of kind G. However such laws are to be formulated in the domain of physical science, but they are rare in other fields like social sciences. Quite often probabilities laws are invoked as explanatory laws in order to explain social situations, human decisions, actions etc. Even though an important corollary of the covering-law theory implies that explanation and prediction have similar structures, it is not customary to apply covering laws in case of human actions. Prediction would be possible in case of human actions if there is the knowledge of all the relevant premises required for the explanandum. A covering law theory may be considered to be too wide. Consider the following explanation having covering law model.

All copper expands when heated.

This piece of copper did not expand.

∴ It is not heated.

In this valid argument it is odd to say that the premises constitute explanans for the conclusion i.e. explanandum, because the negative statement 'this piece of copper is not heated' is not an event-proper to be explained (explanandum). However explanation systematises separate events under a lawful pattern i.e. to say that explanation is a *rational reconstruction*.

B: It is necessary to modify the covering-law model in order to make it more adequate so that it will be extended to teleological explanation of human actions by rational agents Normally rational actions are goal directed or value oriented; consequently they carry an indirect teleological implication. Since human beings are not just physical or mindless biological entities, their nature is likely to be influenced and modified by culture. But even if it is necessary to consider motives and intentions ; human beings make plans and their actions are determined by a goal they seek to achieve. Consequently it is necessary to workout subjective and objective laws. Laws governing human action may not in a simpler form but complex one. Even authors like Hempel slightly modify their position by way of saying "If X is a man, then given conditions C, he will do *a* is more restrictive sort because it is necessary to consider 'if x is a man who is l, m, n, then given c, he will do a". However it is necessary to articulate, l,m. n, etc. in order to provide adequate deductive structure for scientific explanation. As an alternative to deductive model it may be argued that universal hypothesis i.e. a law-like statement is not a requirement so that there is no need of deducibility, there are only assessments or judgements as guiding threads for conducting human actions. However even assessments and judgements presuppose laws. For instance in historical explanation it is necessary to state general laws based on regularity. Some time probabilities and statistical laws play the role of general statements, however in that case the explanandum is only probable but no longer deducible from the explanans. Any restatement of causal model implies the formulation of non-trivial laws including initial conditions of rational agents.

The statements concerning human events are to be deduced from the principles governing the behaviour of the participating individuals and description of their situations because human actions as form of social phenomenon is autonomous. Consequntly there is a need of macroscopic analysis of human events. Normally human actions are structured in teleological frame work, there is the necessity of the criteria to identify purposive activity. A behavioural criterion of C_1 purposive activity i.e goal directed activity^{c1}"consists in persistence and sensitivity toward the goal under varying conditions. For clearer understanding of the criterion it is necessary to consider the nature of purposive activity (d1). "An activity is purposive if and only if it exhibits sensitivity and persistence toward a goal as a result of directive correiation". The technical expression directive-correlation implies that two variables such as the position of a moving target and the direction in which an automatic target-tracking mechanism are directly correlated with respect to the goal. I wish to modify the above definition of purposive activity including the directive-correlation. Since purposive activity or goal directed activity involves intentions of rational agents; it is necessary to incorporate the intentional elements in the definiens. And an automatic target-tracking mechanism is to be replaced by rational agent because human beings with appropriate intentions execute voluntarily their actions. Accordingly (d_2)" an activity is purposive (i.e. voluntary or rational) if and only if it is the rational agent who has the adequate intention combined with successful execution toward a goal." Since purposive activities belong to the agents who deliberately undertake courses of action for the sake of consciously envisaged (goal); it is necessary to work out a new model for explaining the human actions. Above criterion (c1) of purposive activity, modified in conformity with d2 (modification of d1), implies that agent's intentions, corresponding behavioural traits, capacity for successful execution of an act combined with teleological general laws provide an adequate explanation for human act (i.e. rational act).

NOTES

1. Human actions are broadly classified under two categories (a) voluntary actions and (b) involuntary actions. Voluntary actions as rational actions are considered to be purposive or goal directed acts. Normally human actions are in the form of movements of an individual. Subject's behaviour consists of series of his movements with or without intentions. Voluntary actions if explpined properly, give rise to adequate understanding of human situations.

2. Every rational action presupposes reasons or grounds for why it was performed instead of an alternative act. But reasons for given act may be adequate or inadequate. Even if adequate reasons for a given act are traced there might be another level of moral evaluation of that act. Consequently moral acts presuppose rational acts. And rational acts are also subject to aesthetic evaluation.

3. Hempel's (1965:469) contention is to modify Dry's principle of rational action. However an adequacy of such modification may be questioned, because of certain syntactical and semantical peculiarities of teleological sentences. The language of natural events and the language of human actions have their own boundaries.

4. It is also necessary to inquire into a possible explanation for a negative explanandum say 'A did not do X'. If A did not do X then either A did some Y other than X or he did not do anything at all. In either case there is a necessity to provide explanans. But an explanans of one may not be the same as that of the other.

5. Even if Davidson is right in showing the falsity of an empirical law in Hempel's schema, he is not justified to refute the schema as invalid because it is possible for a valid schema to have one or more false premises along with true conclusion.

6. Davidson (1985:5), in this context is unclear regarding the distinction between reason and function of a reason. It is not difficult to show the structural differences between them, for instance reasons or grounds (i.e. premises) need not cause certain conclusion which is only deducible. Normally causality functions in the empirical domain, where as reason covers even non-empirical formal domains such as formal logic.

7. However laws are also subject to explanation by way of subsuming less general laws under more general laws. Kepler's laws of planetary motion are explained by more general law of gravitation. In scientific theory observational terms are derived from observable features of the world; where as experimental laws are derived from theoretical laws.

8. See 'Holism and individualism' (by W.H.D) in Encyclopeadia of Philosophy, ed. by P. Edwards, Vol. IV, p. 53 Collier MacMillan, I.C., New York. Holism implies that social phenomenon is autonomous and hence needs macroscopic analysis. However micro-analysis of human acts must be integrated to macro analysis. Human acts in a large contexts of social phenomenon are to be analysed even with reference to other factors like natural environ mental set up, and individual's potentialities to achieve his desired goal. Thus careful consideration of subjective elements and objective factors is necessary for proper understanding of human acts.

BIBLIOGRAPHY

1. Anscombe, G.E.M. (1976) : *Intention*, Basil Blackwell, Oxford.
2. Aristotle (1949) : *Ethica Nichomachean*, Translatated by W.D. Ross, Oxford.
3. Brandt R. (1989) : 'Practical Rationality', in *Philosophy and Phenomenological Research*, Vol. 1,) No. 1 pp. 125-30.

4. Danto, A.C. (1973) : *Analytical Philosophy of Action*, Cambridge University Press.

4. Davidson, D. (1975) : *Essays on Actions and Events*, Clarendon Press, Oxford.

5. Hempel, C.G. (1965) : *Aspects of Scientific Explanation*, Collier, MacMillan Ltd., London.

6. Hudson, W.D. (1970): *Modern Moral Philosophy*, MacMillan and Co., London.

3

THE STRUCTURE OF ACTION SENTENCES

1. The action sentences are about human actions. But how to formalise action sentences, used in conversational (or ordinary) language, for adequate clarification of the notion of human action ? How are we to assess the alternative formalisations posed by the authors like Reichenback, (R) Davidson (D) and others ?

2. Davidson's (D) (1985:115-120) reaction to Reichenbach (R) (1966 : 266:274) is as follows :

Davidson (115) thinks that according to Reichenbach we may transform a sentence like :

(i) 'Amundsen flew to the North pole' into :

(ii) (∃x) (x consists in the fact that Amundsen flew to the North Pole).

Here the expression 'is an event that consists in the fact that' is to be viewed as an operator. R thinks that (i) ≡ (ii) and (ii) has its counterpart in ordinary idiom :

(iii) A flight by Amundsen to the North Pole took place. Thus (i) and (iii) are two expressions for the same idea expressed in (ii). But (i) and (iii) have quite different logical forms yet logically equivalent. (Syntactically : different and semantically same.) But (D says this will not do) Following R we translate :

(iv) 'Amundsen flew to the North Pole in May 1926.' into :

(v) (∃x) (x consists in the fact that Amundsen flew to the North Pole in May 1926).

According to Davidson correct way to render (iv) is :

(vi) (∃x) (x consists in the fact that Amundsen flew to the North Pole and x took place in May 1926).

(vi) alone is the logical form of (iv) for Davidson.

*Davidson also raises two objections to R's analysis of action sentences** (a1:) R's analysis may be applied to any sentence whatsoever, whether it deals with actions, events or anything, else. For instance '2+3=5' becomes '(∃x) (x consists in the fact that 2+3=5)', further '(∃y) (y consists in the fact (∃x) (x consists in the fact that 2+3=5)' and so on. Thus it is not clear on what principle the decision to apply the analysis is based.

(a2) : Following inference is incorrect :

(vii) (∃x) (x consists in the fact that I flew my spaceship to the Morning Star).

(viii) The Morning Star = the Evening Star

∴ (ix) (∃x) (x consists in the fact that I flew my spaceship to the Evening Star).

D's Solution : (*118-9* : Verbs of action that say 'what someone did' should be construed as containing a place for singular forms; following is the correct from :

(x) (∃x) (Flew (I, my spaceship, x) and To (the Morning Star, x).

(xi) = (viii) the Morning Star = the Evening Star

∴ (xii) (∃x) (Flew (I, my spaceship, x) and To (the Evening Star, x)

Davidson thinks that in R's analysis there seems no clear principle on which to refrain from applying the analysis to every sentence.

3. In order to assess D's claim and D's presentation of R's view it is necessary to present R's actual position. For precise understanding of R's position regarding the formalization of action sentences. I would like to paraphrase R's position in section 48 to which D refers. R makes the distinction between individuals of *thing type* like the human body aggregates of matter keeping together for a certain time and individuals of *event type* which are merely space-time coincidences, (as in theory of relativity) which do not endure). Even though such distinction is more fundamental in theory of relatively, the alleged distinction is

also made in conversational language—because sometimes events are also considered as important for the purposes of daily life. Events of coronation, a travelling, an election occur in daily life. Normally such events as designated by means of *individual descriptions* but not by proper names. For example 'the coronation of George VI took place at Westminster Abbey'. This sentence involves two term relation between an event and a thing. Even though it is frequently possible to eliminate event sentences like 'George VI was crowned at W.A.', there are some relations which can be formulated only as relations between events such as time-sequences and causality and hence such sentences cannot be reduced to thing types of sentences. *R* thinks of irreducibility of event sentences to thing type of sentences. R introduces the term *situation* to designate the object corresponding to a proposition. He shows that there are two ways of splitting a *situation* ; as thing—Splitting and event splitting. In the tautological equivalenəe if f(x1)≡g (v1) [when 'vi' denotes the event and 'g' event property), if 'f (x1) means 'George VI is crowned, 'g' is the predicate coronation. Further, use of *asterisk* indicates transition to event splitting so that the function 'g' takes the form [f (x1)];* consequently 'g (v1)' ≡ [f (x1)]* (v1)'.

V_1 (as definite description) = (iv) [f (xi)]* (V). The event is indicated by a bound variable 'v'. This mode of expression is prevalent in conversational ordinary language in order to use such predicates as 'takes place', 'occurs' which express existence. Thus 'the coronation of George VI took place' is represented as :

(v) [f (x1)* (v)].

For a given thing—function (f) there are different ways to construct fact-functions. For instance the sentence 'Amundsen flew to the North Pole in May 1926', is to be symbolized in *thing-splitting* by

f(x1, Y1, t1) which can be transformed into *event-splitting* in *different* ways.

(iii) (∃x) [f(x1, Y1, t1)* (v) where f (x1, Y1, tl) stands for the fact function: '*Amundsen's flight to the North Pole in May 1926*' And (i) reads as : a flight by Amundsen to the North Pole in May

1926 took Place'. By using another fact-function '[f (x1, y1)] the following form is obtained :

(xiv) (∃v) [f (x1, y1)] (V1 t1) which can be read as 'a flight by Amundsen to the North Pole took place in May 1926. Further the fact function' [f (x1)*] yields the form :

(xv) (∃v) [f(x1)]* (v1, y1. t1), which stands for : 'one of Amundsens flights took place at the North Pole in May 1926'. Events, like things, are also carriers of properties.

4. Now let me consider D's interpretation of R. D thinks that (iv) is to be correctly rendered as (vi) but not as (v). But R considers (vi)=(xiv) as one of the forms of (iv) along with (xiii) and (xv). Further D's formulisation is only partial (vi) unlike (xiv) consists of many unsymbolized expressions.

Answer to (a_1) : R's analysis of action sentences cannot be applied to any sentence whatsoever because of the criterion of irreducibility namely an event type sentence is irreducible to a thing type sentence if there are relations between events such as *time*, *sequence* and *causality*. Consequently sentence like '2+3=5' are to be excluded from event type of sentences.

(a2) is correct inference because the conclusion necessarily follows from the premises. Using R's symbolising techniques a2 may be symbolised as follows :

(a3)	1.	(∃y) [(f (x, y, t)] (v). .	(A (space-ship) flight by me took place to Morning Star).
	2.	y=z . .	(Morning Star=Evening Star)
∴	3.	(∃z) [f (x, z, t)] (v) . .	(A (space-ship) flight by me took place to Evening Star).

The Rule of identity permits to draw (3) from (1) and (2).

Using Copi's symbolisation, a_2 is to be symbolised as :

(a_4)	1.	F im	F im = I flew to m
	2.	m=e	
∴	3.	Fie	m = Morning Star
	4.	Fie 1.2. Identity	e = Evening Star

5. R has considered one type of event sentences as action sentences involving existential quantifier (∃x); however there are general action sentences and singular action sentences involving universal quantifier (x) and (ix) (Fn)—as definite descriptions. It has been a general practice among the writers of modern logic to treat action sentences in the sections of (a) propositional logic, quantifier logic and logic of relations including identity and definite descriptions. Let me draw some examples for each type from Copi's symbolic logic (1973).

(a) Either Atlanta *wins* their conference championship and Baltimore *wins* their conference championship or a Chicago *wins* the superbowl (Copi : 13).

In this compound action sentence the action term '*wins*' occurs thrice as marked above. And the sentence is to symbolized as : (A.B) VC.

This kind of formalisation dose not provide specific syntactical structures of action sentences because of common propositional functions for action and non-action (indicative) sentences.

(b) If anything is *discovered* someone will be honoured.
[Dx=x is discovered

Px=x is a person

x=x will be honoured]

The symbolic formula is :

(x) [Dx] (y) [y) [Py. Hy]

There are two action terms : '*discovering*' and '*honouring*'.

(c) 'Plato *taught* Aristotle' is to be the sentence symbolised as : *Tpa*.

Just as in case of (a) even in (b) and (c) there are common schema for action and non-action (indicative) sentences. *But the question is* how are we to specify the structures of actions sentences used in (a), (b) and (c) ? Is there any unique property in action sentences in contradistinction with non-action (indicative) sentences even though they share common propositional functions ? As seen above, R thinks of special syntax for action sentences. On

R's, syntactical analysis, criterion of demarcation of action sentences from non-action sentences is in the form of irreduability criterion of action sentences to non-action sentences through temporal factor because action occurs at a definite point of time. However time factor (t) is not incorporated in Copi like formulations. Following R, D also recognises *temporal factor* in action sentences. It is to be noted that *R's syntax to action sentences* accommodates any action sentence whether it is about human action or natural action in the form of an event.

6. Now the question is 'What is the nature of a sentence' pertaining to human action and to how are we to define such a sentences ? S as a sentence about human action may be defined as "x is an action sentence = df x consists of an *action term* pertaining to human action".

Since the definiens consists of a key (form) i.e '*action term*' (t) is necessary to inquire, into the logical status of 'action term' for clearer understanding of an *action sentence.*

What is an action term ? Normally action term refers to an action. And an action term is either a verb namely (to walk, to type, to fly, to climb etc.) or a verbal-noun (or gerund) derived from the corresponding verbs (namely Walking, typing, flying, climbing etc). Usual distinction between transitive and intransitive verbs may not be extended to nouns and adjectives. Transitive verbs represent one place functions like 'x walks', 'x swims' etc; which are structurally similar to 'x is blue', 'x is tall' etc. 'Devadatta walks' is to be symbolised as 'Wd'. 'Devadatta is tall' as 'Td'.

However the transitive verbs take two place-functions like 'x gives y', 'x helps y' etc. Transitive verbs are also used in three place, four-place or n-place functions. The sentence 'Peter sends a telegram to Paul' involves three place functions. However 'x helps y' ≠ 'y helps x' unless x=y. If x ≠ y, 'x helps y' = 'y is helped by x'. There are also instances where actions terms take the places of variables e.g. 'pressing the switch causes ringing the bell' this sentence has the binary function 'x causes y'. Similarly 'typing is faster than writing' has also binary function.

Action terms are either singular or general; a singular term like 'the discovery of Radium'. 'The first landing on the moon' etc. refer to single human act. Terms like 'voting', 'walking', 'jumping', 'helping' 'cooking' etc are general action terms because each expression refers to any number of token acts coming under a given type of act. Action terms if refers to natural acts like walking, eating, running, they may be called as natural action terms, however if action terms are called artificial or non-natural action terms if they refer to such artificial acts like 'manufacturing, 'driving', 'Phonning' etc.

7. *Action terms as rigid designators :* According to the theory of rigid designator, singular terms or proper names and general names are considered to be rigid designator because such terms refer to the corresponding referents, in every conceivable state of affairs (i.e. possible worlds). However at present the theory of rigid designator ,accommodates only singular names or proper names and natural kind terms, artifact terms and mass terms. Now the question is whether action terms are also rigid designators ?

According to the definition of rigid designator : "x is a rigid designator = df x refers to its referent (object) in every possible world, if it exists". Rigid designator seems to apply only in case of the domain of objects where an object is not an event. Further individuals and natural kinds are relatively more durable than events or actions. However exponents of the theory of rigid designator are hopeful about the extension of the theory to action terms, because they have made (implicit) claim that any term whether it is a noun or verb is a rigid designator. Consequently verbal-nouns are also rigid designators. According to the theory of rigid designation every referring expression, especially all names (and also some definite descriptions) are rigid designators, and action terms as nouns refer to actions; hence action terms are also rigid designators. Accordingly, given an action term *t*, the referring relation between *t* and the corresponding action *a* is always rigid in the sense that *t* always refers to *a* wherever *a* accurs; action a is a bearer of its name *t* in every possible state of affair where it exists or occurs or happens. However an unnamed or unknown action is not a bearer of action term even though it is capable of doing so only after naming it by an action term. Since theory of rigid designation, in case of proper names and natural kind terms, implies essences in the form of necessary properties of individual and natural kinds; it is desirable to inquire into the essential properties implied by action sentences containing action terms as rigid designators.

Analysis of action sentences normally consists of singular action terms containing definite description or singular term and a general sentence involves action term in the form of general term or common noun. General action terms are usually generated from the corresponding verbs; action terms like 'writing', 'greeting', 'driving' etc. are derived from the corresponding verbs : 'to write', 'to greet' and 'to drive'. If action terms are treated as rigid designators as shown above; then action sentences exhibit certain logical properties as shown below.

Consider a general action sentence like '*Typing is a form of writing*'. In this sentence there are two action terms namely 'typing' and 'writing'. The verb 'is' functions as a set membership relation, accordingly the set of all the acts of typing is a subset of the set of all the acts of writing; symbolically $T \in W$ (T= acts of typing, W=acts of writing; C stands for 'is a set of'). Parallel to Putnam's analysis of ostensive definition of natural kind term—water namely 'this is water', it is possible to consider ostensive definition for action term--'typing' namely 'this is typing'. In this ostensive definition the indexical term 'this' designates a particular act (i.e. token act) i.e. to say that 'this is typing' means 'this act is an act of typing'. Normally the word 'this' in the above sentence designates a given act of typing in the actual world. Further given an orbitrary act (of writing) in any possible world, in order that the given act is an act of typing it must be the same type of act as this in the actual world. In other words, If a_1 is an act of writing in any possible world (W), a_2 is an act of typing in the actual world (Wa) and a_1 is the same type of act as a_2 in the actual world then a_1 is also an act of typing. Consequently something is an act of typing (a_1) in any possible world (W) if and only if it (a_1) is the same type of act as a_2 (in W (a) designated by *this*. If the compound word 'the same type act' stands for cross world relations then following symbolization for the ostensive definition may be given.

1. (W) (X) (Exists (x)—→[π typing (x) ←——→ same (x in w, this W Σ] (Here w is a possible world, W(a) is the actual world, x is an individual variable, 'Exists (x)' refers to x is an act of typing in W; 'same'τ 'means same type of act).

For precise articulation of the ostensive definition, it is desirable to give a precise formulation of 1. i e. symbolic formulation of the ostensive definition for given act of typing. In the above formulation (1) expressions : 'X in W' and 'this in-W(a)' denote events across the possible world. But this view may seems to go against the temporal characteristics of human actions as species of temporal events at physical level. In other words, it seems to be odd to understand a given action across the possible worlds because actions are unlike enduring objects or individuals. In reply to this criticism it may be said that even though actions as events have short duration compared to other things or persons, nevertheless actions do exist so that they may be perceived. Thus one can stipulate a possible existence or occurrence of an act in any possible state-of-affair. However non modal version (1) of an ostensive definition might be given as :

2. (x)[(π typing (x)←——→con-specific (x, this)].

This formula stands for "Something is an act of typing if and only if it is a member (token) of the same type of act as *this*". In the con-specific relation a pair of individual events x and y are said to be *con-specific* if and only if x is a member of the given type class (or species) that y or *this* is a member of accordingly following is this conspecific relation :

3. Conspecific (x_1 y)=df. x E(1z) [Species (type) (z) YEZ].

By making use of con-specific relation (3) the precise formulation of (1) takes the following form 1 :

4. (W) (X) [Exists_W(X)—→ $(^{\pi}\text{Typing}_W(\times)$←——→$\times E_u$ (1z)

[Type_{Wa}(z) this EW_a Z])].

In ordinary English (4) stand for :

For every possible world *W*, something happening in *W* is

an act of typing in *W* if and only if it is a member in *W* of the same type of acts that *this* is a member of in the actual world.

It is somewhat interesting to apply K and I mechanisms to human actions in order to consider the possibility of generating necessary aposteriori statements about actions. K-mechanism helps to generate necessary a posteriori propositions about kind or type of acts where as I mechanism is about individual action sentences. Let me consider following action sentences pertaining to scientific acts, namely (i) synthesis of water is the act of chemical combination of hydrogen and oxygen; (ii) testing of Boyle's Law of gas is the act of increasing or decreasing the pressure of a given volume of a gas. There are also individual action sentences about specific single act such as : (iii) The discovery of Radium is the investigation of a radioactive element and (iv) The discovery of electron is the investigation of negatively charged sub-atomic particle. According to the theory of direct reference (i) to (iv) are considered to be necessary aposteriori statements because in every statement both subject and predicate are rigid designates and also co referential. Consequently such statements sustain counter factual situations, that is to say that if a sentence containing rigid desinators is true on the basis of empirical discovery in the actual world then they continue to be true in every possible world or possible state of affair. In the above examples (i) to (iv) subject and predicate terms are definite descriptions, nevertheless they are rigid designators because they refer to the same act in every possible state-of-affair. However action terms like 'typing', 'synthesising', testing, 'analysing' etc. are of general character referring to any number of singular acts coming under the given category or class of actions. Each action kind term implies definite and indefinite descriptions of which a given act may be individuated. Normally individating descriptions are definite descriptions The description 'a form of writing' is an indefinite or general form for it refers to typewriting, handwriting, etc. In other words 'typing' is a species of writing. However there must be specific functions involved in typing in virtue of which that act is to be qualified as an act of typing but not any other act. Thus typing involves specific functions. Consequently in any possible state of affair essential function of a given act like typing remains the same. The theory of rigid designation seems to imply essentialism. Consequently it is possible to derive essential characteristics of actions from action terms as rigid designators. However it is necessary to examine such a claim. *K-mechanism* normally consists of three component premisses : the ostensive definition, the statement of essential characteristic of a given act based on careful observation and a general essentialist premiss. The three premisses together imply the conclusion in the form of necessary aposteriori statement.

I wish to consider the possibility of generating necessary aposteriori statements pertaining to voluntary acts. Putnam and Donnellan's scheme for generating necessary aposteriori statements may be extended to action statements as shown below.

The mechanism consists of three premises : (i) the ostensive definition of an action term which rigidly designates the corresponding act, (ii) the statement of about the actual hidden nature of the paradigm mentioned in the definition of action term and (iii) the general principle : Being a sample or an instance of the same class (type) as something consists in having the same (micro) functions Consequently O.K. mechanism suggests the following modal argument.

(a_1)

1. It is necessarily the case that : something is an act of typing if and only if it is an instance of dthat (the same class of acts that *this* is an instance of).
2. *This* (act) has the hidden nature as specific function (f).
3. Being an instance of the same class of acts as something consists in having the same specific function (f).

Therefore

4. It is necessarily the case that : every act of typing has the specific function (f).

In this argument premiss 1 does not seem to be an exact formulation of the ostensive definition of a given act of typing. Usually ostensive definition of a given act of typing takes the form : 'This is an act of typing'. However second premiss is straight forward.

The complex nature of the third premiss raises certain difficulties and one of them is that, it (3) (already) presupposes the conclusion(4). I think it is also possible to give a non-modal version of (al) as follows :

(a_2)

1. This is an act of typing.
2. This (act) has the specific function (f).
3. This act as an instance of the class of typing acts consists of the same specific function(f).

Therefore

4. Every act of typing has the specific function(f).

In order to examine the validity (a1) and (a2) it is necessary to consider the question: does the conclusion necessarily follow from the premisses? Both the conclusion of a_1 and a2 are universal general statements. Therefore there must be at least one universal premiss in each argument so that the respective conclusion necessarily follows from the premisses in conformity with the rules of valid inference.

Normally scientific generalisations are established on the basis of the observations of sample particulars belonging to a certain kind or type. While formulating scientific laws as statements of general facts, often inductive strategy works in scientific investigations but not deductive machinery as shown in (al) and (a2). It is hard to believe if an empirical science makes use of deductive mode of reasoning followed in (al) and (a2) in order to formulate scientific laws or theories Usually formal sciences like logic and arithmetic are said to be deductive in nature, for on the basis of accepted axioms (or postulates) and definitions certain formulas are deductively derived from the system of axioms and definitions in conformity with rules of valid inference. In view of such consideration O.K. mechanism seems to be either circular or deductively incorrect. Circularily is due to the assumptions of the conclusion as third premiss. Even if the third premiss and the conclusion are considered to be different, the question about the material correct-ness and justification of the third premiss arises; however such a premiss cannot be considered to be an analytic sentence but it must be empirical one. If the general statement is empirical it must be based on other empirical statements. Supporting empirical statements might be either particular or general. If supporting statements are particular then the justification of general statement is inductive. On the other hand if the justifying statement is general then there is deductive justification. But deductive justification may lead to infinite regress because c1 is deduced from c2 and c2 from c3, and c3 from c4 and so on. Of course inductive justification itself raises some other issues like the validity of inductive justification which is non-deductive. Even though authors like Popper have made an attempt to give deductive justification for inductive scientific laws through his theory of falsification, such an attempt is hardly convincing. Because basically scientific B inquiry is both inductive and deductive. Human reasoning in general is inductive. Consequently in the rationalisation of human acts both deductive and inductive patterns of thought play their roles for clearer understanding of the nature of acts.

While understanding the nature of human acts two different questions may be asked : (i) What is the structure of human acts and (ii) How are we to explain human acts ? However the structure of action sentences provide a scheme for understanding the nature of human acts. Thus the analysis of action language helps to understand actions. If action language is cognitive in nature then action sentence is a bearer of truth value. Consequently a true action sentence describes the action as a fact. But are actions facts ? If actions are also facts, how are they distinguished from other facts which are non-acts? The criteria which emerges from the structural explication of human act provides criterion of demarcations to distinguish between acts and non-acts. Human acts are the species of events in general, because an act is that which occurs or happens. However there exist facts or states of affairs without being occurred. Actions as events are also considered to be states-of-affairs, because they are described through cognitive language. Consequently actions are also subject of explanation the manner in which natural events are explained. Normally rational acts are subject to explanation in terms of motivating reasons.

REFERENCES

1. Copi, I.M. (1973) : *Symbolic Logic*, MacMillan Co., New York.
2. Davidson, D. (1985) : *Essays on Actions and Events*, Clarendon Press, Oxford.
3. Grayling, A.C. (1982) : *An Introduction to Philosophical Logic*, The Harvester Press, Sussex.
4. Kalish, D.R., Montague and Garyman (1980) : *Logic : Techniques of Formal Reasoning*, Jovanovich, Inc. N.Y. London.
5. Kripke, S. (1984) : *Naming and Necessity*, Basil, Blackwell, Oxford.
6. Linsky, L. (1977) : *Names and Descriptions*, The University of Chicago Press, Chicago, London.
7. Putnam, H. (1975) : *Mind, Language and Reality*, Cambridge University Press, Cambridge.
8. Quine, W.V.O. (1972) : *Methods of Logic*, Halt Reinehart, New York.
9. Reichenbach, H. (1947) : *Elements of Symbolic Logic*, MacMillan Co., New York.
10. Salmon, N.U. (1984) : *Reference and Essence*, Basil Blackwell, Oxford.

4

KNOWLEDGE OF VOLUNTARY ACTION IN NAVYA-NYĀYA

1. The concept of kṛti as voluntary action plays a cardinal role in Navya-Nyāya ethics, because, voluntary actions are morally evaluated. That is to say that ethical discourse presupposes the concept of kṛti (voluntary action). For adequate understanding of the notion or kṛti it is necessary to consider the questions (i) What is kṛti? (ii) What are the conditions of kṛti (voluntary action). Thus the aim of this paper is to explicate the notion of kṛti as voluntary action in terms of contemporary ideas.

2. Every voluntary action is performed by the agent, or the man acts voluntarily if actions are generated in him According to Annaṃbhaṭṭa[1] (1700 A.D.) "The agent is one who possesses three things namely intimate cognizance of the material cause, a will to act, and an effort". Accordingly the three attributes jñāna (knowledge), icchā (desire) and prayatna (effort) are causally related to each other. Consequently there cannot be an effort unless there is a will and a will to do can only arise if there is previously apprehended material cause on which the will is to function, kṛti being the final stage, it necessarily presupposes knowledge and will pertaining to feasibility of action To this effect Viśvanāth[2] (17th century) thinks that just as cutting instruments such as an axe cannot produce any result without an agent, similarly the eyes and other instruments of knowledge cannot produce result without an agent. Thus an agent is inferred.

Normally an activity is that which brings into being an object to be produced so that whatever comes into being is also brought into being which is designated by the nominative case of the verb 'to be'. An activity of the agent towards the course of action terminates in a result. In case of imperatives the activity of an agent is conveyed by a verb, for instance we grasp the act of cooking etc. from the verbs 'cooks', 'goes' etc. Consequently we make out the activity of an agent who is connected with the acts. The meaning of the verb 'cooks' implies one who does the act of cooking which becomes the object of the transitive verb 'does'. The action sentence 'pākam karoti' is semantically equivalent to 'pacati'. The word 'pāka' is derived from the root 'pac' and it gets the second case-ending (dvitiya-vibhakti-pratyaya). Consequently this case ending points to the fact that paka is the object of 'karoti'. Thus the verb 'karoti' (does) designates the activity of an agent. Both the action sentences, 'Devadatta does cooking' and 'Devadatta cooks' are logically equivalent, for both anwser the question 'What does Devadatta do' in the same manner.[3]

3. It is to be noted that generally all transitive verbs having terminal inflexions refer to the activity of an agent. Of course actions can be individuated with reference to specific action terms. For instance 'he cooks', 'he reads' etc. reveal the specific nature of actions. Normally an agent chooses a rational course of action in pursuit of given ends. And in that case he must take into account relevant available information concerning particular circumstance in which the action is to be taken, different means by which the given ends might be attained. Thus it is desirable to inquire into the necessary and sufficient conditions of voluntary action.

In Navya-Nyāya especially (in) Viśvanātha's[4] *Bhāṣā-pariccheda* (V. 149) and *Siddhānta Muktāvalī* we find the following conditions of voluntary action.

D1 : An act a is voluntary if and only if (i) the agent of an act *a* desires to do a (ii) he knows that he can do *a* (iii) he also knows that an act *a* is conducive to him and (iv) he also knows the instruments or the means of doing *a*. For adequate understanding of D1 it is necessary to analyse the key notions like desire (icchā), intention (cikīrṣā) etc. Desire may be relating to the result of an act or it may be regarding to the means of action. The result of an act is in the form of pleasure and absence of pain. However prior knowledge of the result of an act is the cause of a desire for that result. Thus happiness can be the object of human pursuit for that which being known is desired as belonging to oneself is the object of human life. This kind of characterisation of the pursuit human beings reminds us Mill's utilitarianism But there are fundamental differences, because utilitarianism implies empirical happiness where as Nyāya theory implies spiritual summum bonum. Normally the desire for the happiness arises from the prior knowledge of it.[5]

Next the concept of cīkīrṣā is quite relevant for the explication of action because only when an agent possesses a specific state of mind then only he will be inclined to do the desired act. Visvanatha[6] defines cikīrṣā (as the desire to do) is that wish (for an action) in which feasibility through one's effort is feature. Accordingly cikirṣā is a desire (iccha) however every form of desire need not be cikirṣā, because cikirṣā is a special type of action oriented desire in which there is a belief regarding the feasibility of an act through one's own effort. The notion of cikīrṣā may capture the sense of intention of an act. Intention of a voluntary act is a necessary condition prior to the execution of an act; it consists of propsitional non-propositional elements like belief, volition etc. relevant for doing a particular act.

The desire to do i.e. cikīrṣa is that wish having feasibility through one's effort as its feature relating to an action. For instance, cikīrṣa is expressed through a sentence having the form. 'I shall effect cooking through (my) effort.[7]' An action sentence always presupposes the prior intention to be expressed in the form of a sentence 'k intended to do y'r 'k had belief regarding his own capacity for cooking'. Since the cause of the desire to do is the notion of feasibility through one's effort, there is no desire to do regarding natural events like raining etc. Because there is the absence of the notion of their feasibility through one's effort.[8] Thus, the following inference is valid.

1. If there is the absence of awareness regarding feasibility through one's effort to do then there is no desire to do *a*.
2. There is the absence of awareness regarding feasibility through an effort to cause raining.
3. ∴ There is no desire to cause raintall.

In other words.

1. If an agent knows that he cannot do *a* then he cannot desire to do a.

2. Natural events like raining cannot be caused by human agents.

3. ∴ Human agents cannot desire to cause natural events.

However the absence of desire is also caused by non-conducive effects of an act. Thus an agent cannot express his desire to eat food mixed with honey and poison as it is not good for his health, so he avoids it. Thus there is a need of absence of negative condition in order to have an appropriate intention. In this context the method of agreement and difference is employed.[9] The method implies that there are two sets namely positive set of intentions and negative set of intentions. A positive set of intention is characterised by the presence of desire to do an act a through one's effort if it is conducive to an agent; however in case of negative set there is a withdrawal or abstaining from a desire to do an act if it is not conducive to the agent. Therefore an agent forms an intention if he knows that action is feasible and also the result of action is conducive to him.

4 However Prābhākara of Pūrva-Mīmāṃsā[8]—raises objections against the Nyāya view that the notion of conduciveness is the cause of inclination (pravrtti). He argues that if it is the case that the notion of conduciveness to what is desirable is the cause of inclination then there would be an inclination for an act like bringing down the lunar orb since it is conducive to do so; however that is beyond the capacity of human beings. But Nāiyāyikas reject this contention by saying that if the alleged act is infeasible then there is no question of having a desire for that act whether it is conducive or not. In other words feasible acts are desirable if they are conducive also. Prabhākara encounters Nyāya position by subscribing to his view that the notion of feasibility is alone the cause of inclination; hence it is simpler (lāghava). Otherwise it is cumbrous (gaurava) to postulate additional notion like conduciveness of an act. However on Nyāya view there is no such fallacy and on the contrary it is said that if the Mīmāṃsaka is right then there would be an inclination for eating a food mixed with honey and poison and for saluting a roadside tree, for there is the notion of their feasibility, however this does not happen in case of any normal human being. Thus there is the necessity of

additional condition of conduciveness of an act. The M̄māṃsakā objects to it : it is not so for the cause of inclination is that notion of feasibility caused by the knowledge of a characteristic of one self being in the subject, that is to say that the characteristic is his desire with regard to optional acts undertaken for self-*satisfaction*. Thus optional activities like a sacrifice cooking are undertaken for self-*satisfaction*. It seems to me that Miṃāmsaka also indirectly considers the necessity of conduciveness in the form of self satisfaction. Thus Miṃāmsaka position is not entirely different from Nyāya view regarding the conduciveness of an act. But this type of compromising is not acceptable to the Mimāmsakas, because he argues that conduciveness to what is desirable and feasibility through one effort cannot be apprehended together. Because being an attainable end and being the means are contradictory and that which has not been accomplished is attainable and the means is that which is attainable and the means is that which is arleady accomplished. Further it is not the case that a thing cannot be known by the same person as both as accomplished and un-accomplished at the same tíme. Thus there is an incompatability between the two. However this need not be so as Naiyāyika points out, since the cause of inclination is due to both feasibility of action and its conduciveness, One can have simultaneously the notion of a thing being a means and end also. For example when a man thinks that a certain act like cooking is feasible through his effort then he is inclided to do that act. If he thinks that cooking is feasible through his effort as he desires food, and has knowledge of what goes to make it, and is also in possession of the materials like rice then he is inclined to cook.

5. In the Western context the nature of voluntary action in terms of necessary and sufficient conditions is as follows :

D2 : An act a is voluntary if and only if

(i) an agent x intends to *a*,

(ii) an agent x is not under ignorance,

(iii) an agent is not surprised to do *a*,

(iv) an agent successfully executes his intention to do *a*.

There are conceptual or logical similarities between D1 (P:54) and D2 because desire to do *a* and feasibility of an act a through own effort of D1 imply on intention to do a and successful execution of intention to do *a* of D2 respectively. Further the knowledge of the means to carryout or execute an act a (of D1) implies agents absence of ignorance and surprise of D2. Thus the concept of krti captures the sense of voluntary action.

However there are additional conditions of kṛti in Nyāya system because of epistemological qualifications of kṛti. The knowledge of voluntary action is the blending of propositional and non-propositional aspects of knowing. Because knowing a given act and knowing how to do that act are essential to perform an act. The difference between knowing that and knowing how in case voluntary action may be illustrated by considering the sentences : (S1) X knows that Y does z and (S2) X knows how to do z. Both (i) and (ii) are logically different and (S1) need not imply the (S2). However if X knows how to do z then he knows the act z. Actions are knowable; there are means for knowing them. Prior knowledge of an act is necessary to take the course of action successfully.

NOTES AND REFERENCES

1. *Tarka-Saṃgraha* and *Dīpikā*, by Annaṇbhaṭṭa Verse 17.
2. *Bhāṣā-Prichheda* (B.P.) with *Siddhānta-Muktāvalī* (SM) Verse 47, Edited and Translated by Swami Madhavananda, Adwaita Ashrama, Calcutta, 1977.
3. *Nyāya-Mañjari* of Jayanta-Bhaṭṭa, Translaṭed by J.V. Bhattacharya, Motilal Banarasidass, Delhi, 1978, pp. 704-9.
4. Cikirṣā, kṛti sādyatva prakāreccha . . . tadhetuḥ kṛti sādye iṣtasādhanātvam . . . Bhāṣā-Pariccheda, Vol. 147. Upādānasya cādhyakṣa pravrattau janakam bhavet.
5. B.P. 147, S.M., 241.
6. SM, 147.
7. SM, 147 (i) S.M. 149 and)
8. Madhavananda (op. cit), pp. 243-44.
9. Hudson W.D. : *Modern Moral Philosophy*, MacMillan London, 1970, pp. 333-45.

5

MEANING OF ACTION SENTENCES

Human understanding of action depends on the nature of action language used. Action language pertaining to actions consists of action sentences. Thus, there is a necessity for semantic analysis of action sentences. Both Mimāṃsakas and Naiyāyikas have contributed significant ideas regarding the semantical status of action sentences. Since actions presuppose an agent and consequence of action; there are questions regarding the meaning of an action sentence. Is meaning of an action sentence an action, fruit or consequence of action or an agent of action ? According to one camp an agent is not to be considered as the meaning of a sentence because of divergent views regarding the nature of an agent as signified by a verb. Since uniquence of action sentence is due to action verb, there is a primary consideration of the meaning of action verb. According to Pāṇini's grammar, a lakāra-(a verb) in all its tenses signifies an agent. One may be inclined to say that, a verb in general signifies an agent. However it is argued that an agent of an action is not the meaning of the sentence. Because a verb takes inflexion differently according to the first person (singular and plural) second person and third person. And each number has been indicated by a separate sentence. However Mīmāṃsakas put-forth the hypothesis that activity is the meaning of sentence. There is a close relationship between bhāvanā and activity that it is a form of fruitful activity of the agent towards a course of 'action' yielding a desired result. On careful understanding of a verb like 'to cook' in the present tense reveals that it signifies the activity of an agent. That is to say that we grasp the act of cooking etc. from the verbs 'cooks', 'goes' etc. in order to understand the activity of an agent. It seems to be that action verbs invariably connected with their respective acts. It is to be noted every verb need not designate an action for example in the sentence 'salt is white' the verb does not designate any action. Though acts like cooking etc. are transitory yet the knowledge of the activity of an agent remains unaffected.

The meaning of the verb 'cooks' is normally analysed as one does the act of cooking. Hence the act of cooking is the object of the transitive verb 'does', 'pacati' means 'pākam karoti'. The word 'pāka' is derived from the root 'pac' which gets the second case ending to form the verbal noun 'pākam'. The second case ending designates the fact that pāka is the object of 'karoti' and the word 'karoti' in turn signifies the activity of an agent. The sentences 'Devadatta cooks' and 'he does cooking' have the same meaning, i.e. to say that 'pākam karoti' and 'pacati' have the same meaning. Because the verb 'karoti' is the combination of two elements namely the root kṛ and the terminal inflexion attached to it and the two elements present unified meaning to our consciousness. However it may not be so because two words 'pākam karoti' (he cooks and pacati have different meanings on account of different grammatical configurations. Normally every transitive verb having a terminal inflexion designates the activity of an agent. However certain intransitive verbs do not designate any action but denote existence or being.

Just as cowness belongs to all individualso also there is cows common activity. This common activity is always presented to our consciousness in relation to particular activities. General act (bhāvana) might be considered to be as type-act. And particular acts of a certain kind or type is token act.

There are necessary and sufficient conditions of action: (i) the goal of action i.e. what is to be achieved and (ii) the method or by which means the goal is to be achieved. In case of injunctive sentences containing action verbs, the root and the terminal inflexion are the elements of the verb. And the terminal inflexion in subjunctive moods denotes bhāvana (the mental activity of an agent) because bhāvana refers to a sacrifice (yāga) or any action leading desired result. In other words in a given verb the meaning of root is an object to be achieved and the case ending signifies an asociated object to be achieved. It is said that the meaning of the root say 'yaj' should not be taken as an instrumental case and the inflexion designates an activity to be brought about. However this is not so because the meaning of the root 'yaj' should be taken as an instrumental cause but not as an object, the instrumental cause helps the attainment of an object. For example in the sentence 'agnihotram juhoti' (one should perform the Agnihotra homa), the meaning of the root appears to be the object to be accomplished, as a matter of foct agnihotra is an instrumental cause otherwise the compound word 'svarga kāmaḥ' lacks syntactical relation in the sentence. Whenever an individual is inclined to do certain act, the agent must know how to do it.

Definition or meaning of an injunction (vidhi) : Normally an injunction as an imperative causes a person (an agent) to perform an act However there arise questions like does the suffix as symbol of subjunctive mood cause one to move ? Or whether the function of the awareness of the sense of the suffix gives rise to movement ? It may be replied that there is some super excellent power of an injunction related to the goal. However in the sentence 'svarga kāmo yajet' there no injunctive force like an affirmative sentence. But on listtening an injunction a person pursues the goal; thus persuasive force of an injunction is demonstrated in the attainment of ends by appropriate means. That is to say that injunction is based upon the knowledge of the causal relations holding between an act and the goal of an agent; this knowledge is originated from the awareness of inspiration due to injunction. Consequently meaning of an injunction is the object (goal) achieved by appropriate means. Sentences in subjunctive mood might express Śābda-bhāvana or ārtha-bhāvana. Ārtha-bhāvana is the activity of the agent which causes something to come into being but not denoted by the uninflected verb – "the basic root" Nyāya mañjari (NM) 719) or it is the process denoted by the verb. And śābdabhāvana is that process which belongs to a word or its constituent element which induces an agent to undertake a course of action; this is the view of Kumārila. For example when an agent listens to a sentence containing the verb 'sacrifice' in the subjunctive mood, there two related meanings (i) it is the duty to perform the sacrifice and (ii) that an agent has been induced to do it. Regarding the communication of the meaning of aninjunctive sentence it is generally believed that a meaning of a word is syntactically related to other words in the sentence the presentation of mutually related meanings is called communication. For example, an inflexion of subjunctive mood denotes śābdabhāvanā in the capacity of an injunction and the same inflexion also denotes the inclination of the agent. Hence the mutual relation of these two meanings is presented may be caused as communication. According to Kumārila an injunction enjoins an agent to direct his activity towards a course of action However an inflected verb denotes the senses of both the root of a verb and a suffix attached to it. Both injunction and bhāvanā are presented to the consciousness. Consequently there is no reference to an agent being directed towards a course of action. Completion of an act implies three essential elements, viz. attainment of an end, instrumental cause, the manner of doing it (procedure).

It is replied (NM: 722) that an injunction and the activity of an agent are denoted by one and the same suffix if a bare activity is excited in an agent an injunction may not fulfil the mission. The bhāvanā itself is a complex of many subsidiary elements or accessories. For example the act of cooking consists of so many acts commencing from pouring water into a cooking pot, putting rice into it, the process of boiling and this whole series of acts is known as the act of cooking. Normally the meaning of a sentence is bhāvanā. Some would say that it is the activity which belongs to a word. However the activity of an agent towards a rice is ārthi-bhāvanā and it constitutes the principle meaning of a sentence. It is said that an ārthi-bhāvana is subordinate to śābda-bhāvanā for an activity of an agent is fruitful being a consequence of injunction as śābda-bhāvanā.

Naiyāyikas (seem to) argue that an end is the meaning of an injunctive sentence. A verb normally indicates an end either directly or contextually. Since an end is not an end in itself an agent occupies the main position to derive happiness through a given end.

The injunctive sentences like 'darśapūrrṇamāsābhyām' svarga-kam, yajeta' cause the knowledge of iṣta-sābdabhāsatva in the said act of sacrifice, which is also one of the facts for inducing an agent to undertake an action. Even though such a view is acceptable to Naiyāyikas and Bhāṭṭas, the Prābhākaras do not consider iṣtasābdaphavatva as the meaning of vidhi (imperative) which is only a necessary condition of an action.

In this context it is relevant to consider modern analysis of prescriptive sentences for clear understanding of the nature of moral imperatives. Prescriptivism as a moral theory implies that evaluative language is used "to guide choices" i.e. to say that prescriptive language helps to choose a course of action. For example x wants to guide y to choose to tell the truth; x may do this by using the imperative, tell the truth. In this case x has used a sentence in the imperative mood to prescribe a course of action. Thus an imperative sentence is used to tell someone how to choose his course of action. An ordinary imperative sentence like (i) 'Shut the door' is familiar to ordinary or factual judgement such as : by (ii) "you are going to shut the door". It is said that two sentences have the same propositional content in the form of the same possible state of affairs—as 'your shutting of the door in the next moment. However the two sentences are different because the (i) is neither true nor false but (ii) must be either true or false depending upon the corresponding state of affairs. In ordinary language imperatives are directed towards individuals. Imperatives imply the evaluative notion 'ought', which might be analysed with respect to universal statements as (iii) "all promises ought to be kept"—i.e. "all promises being kept, please".

However this kind of analysis seems to be too narrow for it covers one of the functions of evaluative language i.e. moral discourse; of course there are also ordinary imperatives. There are also non-imperative sentences implying moral facts. It is necessary to understand the imperative in terms of their logical relations. Various attempts have been made to understand the logical status of imperatives in relation to human actions. Mainly the three theories of meaning : The referential theory, verificationist theory and the causal theory are used to interpret imperatives in general including moral imperatives. On referential theory of meaning a given expression in order to be meaningful must refer to certain entity in the world. Accordingly names are meaningful because they name the actual possible or abstract entities in the non-linguistic world. And a sentence turns out to be true if it corresponds to the fact. However in imperatives like 'Devadatta ought to worship god' contain referential expressions like, 'Devadatta', 'God' even the verb 'worship' but the word 'ought' does not seem to correspond to anything in the actual world. For this reason some empiricists (like positivists) deny any cognitive status to the language of imperatives. In other words imperatives or moral judgments are neither verifiable nor falsifiable, for the simple reason that emotive sentence or non-verifiable and imperatives are emotive sentences. However this view has been challenged by Stevenson the foremost exponent of emotivism the subscribed to the causal or psychological theory of meaning. According to that theory it is possible to recognise that it is not enough what language is about but in order to get its meaning we must ask *how* it is about what it is about. Imperatives and moral judgments have a *dynamic character* Stevenson says moral judgments exert "*magnetism*" that is to say that if any one assents to the moral or ethical judgment he must have a tendency to act favourably. Further they create influence also. The causal theory of meaning implies that the meaning of language is its disposition to cause to certain psychological processes in the hearer or speaker. Stevenson's semantics for moral judgments could be extended to the language of imperatives after suitable modifications. Firstly there is a necessity to distinguish between the causal and the logical explanation of language as it has been suggested by Hudson (*Modern moral philosophy* : 44). And then it is possible to establish a relationship between imperatives and factual judgments. Whether a piece of language produces, certain psychological process is a matter of contingent fact, but meaning of language logically depends upon some standard or criterion, hence the logical aspect of action language (of imperatives) cannot be reduced to descrip- tive aspect of that language which is contingent only. Rules of language provide the criterion of meaning for cognitive and non-cognitive language.

So far we have considered critically the nature of action language having cognitive sentences such as 'Devadatta cooks' and imperatives like 'Bring a cow'. Indian semantics provides the same semantical criterion to explicate both the types of action sentences. Thus they differ only in degrees but not in kind. Even though Mīmāṃsakas and Naiyāyikas subscribe different views of meaning, each try to accommodate the action language in their given frame work of meaning. Both the camps subscribe to referential theory of meaning based on appropriate logical and grammatical rules pertaining to syntax and semantics, that is to say for both of them 'Paṇini's grammar is acceptable.' Both of them to try analyse the semantical status of action verbs and normtive elements like 'ought' or 'should' on logical considerations. Nevertheless there are important differences regarding the semantical analysis of actions sentence. For Mīmāṁsakas analysis a verb plays an important role but for Naiyāyikas the role of verb in a given sentence is to co-ordinate with other elements like subject and predicate. It is to be noted that each system provides interesting insights regarding the workings of human language. Consequently we try to get a comprehensive picture of human language regarding its cognitive and non cognitive functions. The basic function of language is its use for the purpose of communication. Human beings communicate facts and also entertain imperatives, for enriching inter personal relations.

NOTES AND REFERENCES

1. Bhattacharya, J.V. (1978, Tr) : *Nyāya-Mañjari* of Jayañta Bhaṭṭā, Motilal, Banarasidass, New Delhi.
2. Jhā, Gangānātha and Dundi Raja Sāstri (Eds) : *Nyāya-Sūtras of Gautam* with Nyāya Bhāsya of Vātsyāyana, Chaukhambha Sanskrit Series, Varanasi.
3. Jha Ganganatha (Tr.) : *Śloka-Vārtika of Kumārila,* Indian Books Centre, Delhi.
4. Jha, V.N. (1986) : *The Logic of Intermediate Causal Link*, Indian Books Centre, Delhi.
5. Feldman, F. (1978) : *Introductory Ethics*, Prentice Hall, India.
6. Hudson, W.D. (1970) : *Modern Moral Philosophy*, MacMillan, London.

6

VOLUNTARY ACTION (KARMA) IN ADVAITA SYSTEM

The notion of voluntary action (karma) plays important role as an aid to jñāna-mārga of Advaita darśana. Since karmayoga is an auxiliary spiritual method to jñāna-yoga, it is necessary to inquire into the nature of karma as voluntary action.

In his Bhagavadgīta-bhāṣya Śaṅkara acknowledges the purport of the verse 16 of chapter IV by saying that 'even the sages of powerful intellects are deluded in respect of the questions what action (work) is and what non-work (inaction) is'. Even though everybody is familiar wtih action, it is not the case that action means exertion or movement of the body and inaction means absence of it i.e. to sit quite. Thus there is the necessity of knowing about good action (karma) which is enjoined by the śāstra (veda), bad action (vikarma) i.e. prohibited action and inaction (akarma). It is to be noted that the word 'karma' in its narrower sense designates good actions only, however in most general usage it designates good action, and bad action and inaction. Eventhough there is incongruence concerning the relationship between action and inaction as incompatable concepts there is a strange solution expressed in the Bhagavad-gīta (IV-18) :

Karmaṇaykarma yaḥ paśyedakarmaṇi ca
karma yaḥ. sa buddhimāna manuṣyeṣu sa
yuktaḥ, kṛtsnakarmakṛt.

"He who can see inaction in action who can also see action in inaction, he is wise among men, he is integrated, he is the performer of all action".

Śri Śaṅkara explicates the notions of action and inaction, by describing that the word 'action' means what is done i.e. an act in general (karmaṇi krīyate iti vyāpāra mātram). Since both inaction presuppose an agent, there is a possibility of seeing inaction in action and action in inaction. Fourther action or inaction, pravṛtti or nivṛtti is related to the agent prior to the self-realization as a means of attaining it. It might be objected that there would be contradiction in action. Action cannot be inaction, they are mutually incompatable. Śaṅkara's reply is as follows :

There is no contradication because from the point of an ignorant man what in reality is inaction appears as action, and what in reality is action appears to be inaction. Accordingly ignorant man wrongly perceives actions and non-actions. Just as actions are wrongly perceived as inactions, good actions might be wrongly perceived as bad karmas (vikarma). Thus in order to understand the distinction between action and inaction, it is necessary to follow the verses 4.17-8 which imply right apprehension of and inaction so that no self-contradiction is involved. And the verse 17 implies that logical distinction of good action, bad action an inaction should be known. Śaṅkara gives an intersting anology that no inaction is contained in action as jujube fruits (in Badari) are contained in a bawl; nor can action be said to be located in inaction, for inaction is the absence of action. An ignorant man is likely to mistake action for inaction and conversely just as he mistakes water in mirage and silver in conch shell. Even though in ordinary life an action and inaction are distinguished form each other there is a possibility of errors just as a man in a moving boat wrongly perceives the stationary tree moving in the opposite direction From spiritual point of view the self is not really an agent (i.e. action-less). Normally human beings are habituated to think of a connection between action with the actionless self, but action pertains to the physical body and mind, however man falsely attributes action to the self by saying that 'I am the agent, mine is action. . .' Similarly there is a possiblity of superimposition on the self the absence of action i.e. inaction which are usually expressed as : 'I do nothing, I rest comfortably'. And in such cases the work of psycho-physical organism remains unchanged but it is super imposed on the eternal self which does not work, however even learned man thinks, 'I work'. In this regard Śri Śaṅkara thinks that the wise man perceives in what others would believe to be work inherent in the self, just as he is aware of the notionless trees despite their apparent movement. Similarly an ignorant man falsely attributes in action to the self because inaction really pertains to the body and the senses consequently there is feelings of happiness and doing nothing. He who understands the distinction between action and inaction is a Yogi.

It may be objected that inaction in action and action in inaction is not a case of illusion but a figurative idea based upon productiveness and unproductivencess of effects. However this is not so. According to Śaṅkara it is not the real purport of the Sūtra, because figurative idea does not serve any purpose that is to say that there is no necessity to mistify the theory of obligatory duties by means of figurative language. "To say that an existent object arises from the non-existent is tantamount to saying that non-existence itself becomes existence and vice-versa, (which is contradiction) . . . He who admits that obligatory duties produce no effects and at the same time holds that they lead to salvation, lands himself in a self-contradiction". Thus Śankara claims that his interpretation is literal and implies the exact sence of the Sūtra 18.

The wise man or the man who has realized the truth performs actions free from desires and purposes, and in worldly life he becomes a best model for others. Whenever a wise man performs actions from spiritual point of view he would do so more effectively; that is to say that a wise man would be more efficient than an ignorant man while performing a given action.

For clearer understanding of the nature of action (karma), it is necessary to consider necessary factors involved in the causation of an action. In the 18th Chapter, verse 14 of Bhagavadgīta explicitly states that the seat (ground), actor (the agent), various organs (as instruments) various functions and the divinity are five factors. According to the bhāṣya of Sri Śankara, the ground or the seat is the body in which attachment aversion etc. arise. The agent (actor) is the delimited self (empirical self) who reaps the fruits of works. The sense-organs are the instruments which apprehend the respective objective objects like sound. Next the manifold movements imply the movements of the vital airs such as in-breath, out-breath etc. The fifth element is the super natural element. For example the solar deity etc, superintend and guide the functions of various sense organs. From the next verse i.e. 15 it is clear that whatever action a man does by the body, speech, and mind, right or wrong these five are the causes of action. The Bhāṣya implies that eventhough they are general causes for an action, there are also special factors in accordance with which an act is considered to be right if it conforms the śāstras. Even though actions are accomplished by the five factors, usually it is said that action is done by means of body mind and speech because consequences are mainly experienced by these means. Further in verse 18 there is a mentioning of three impulses to action namely Knowledge, the object known and the knower. And the organ, the end or purpose and the agent for the basis of action. The Bhāṣya makes it explict that performance of an action to obtain a thing or to avoid another, is possible only if there is a conjunction of the three. There is a relationship between the five causes of action and the three fold basis of action. The organ is that by means which something is done and organs may be external like the organ of hearing etc. and the internal organ like buddhi etc. The end or goal is that which is sought for, or reached through the action by the agent who sets the organs going through the upādhis in which he performs actions.

There are three types of actions. They are sāttvic, rājasic and tāmasic actions (18 : 23-5). An action is sātvic if and only if it is ordained. free from attachment done without love or hatred and one does not desirous of the fruit. An action is rājasic if and only if it is done by one longing for pleasures, and done by egoistic mind. It is to be noted that a realised soul is free from egoitism. However at present the performance of sāttvic action need not be done by realized soul. On the contrary tāmasic action is performed by an ignorant person whose action is under delusion. Normally it is believed that the perfection in karma yoga leads to absolute perfection, that is to say that perfection in karma-yoga consists in being qualified for jñāna-nishṭhā, the path of Wisdom. The supreme state of freedom from action would be attained by a person whose mind or reason (buddhi) is not attached any where and desires are subdued. The knower of the self attains supreme perfection i.e. absolute freedom from action (naiṣkarmya siddhi).

This supreme state is distinguished from the perfection attainable by karma-yoga because it is the state of immediate liberation (sadyo-mukti) and this state is the consequence of right knowledge or renunciation of actions.

There are certain practical hints concerning the performance of actions (Karmas). An agent must have a concern with action alone but never with results or the fruit of action, nor there should be any attachment for inaction (II-47) Because if the agent should have a thirst for the results of works, then he will have to reap them and consequently mental equilibrium might be disturbed. In order to maintain mental balance i.e peace of mind the actions are to be performed in the spirt of detachment. This type of spiritual outlooke helps to develop agent's mental strength also. Sri Śaṅkara thinks that with steadfast in devotion (Yoga) one should perform works for God's sake. Consequently success (Siddhi) in the form of the attainment of knowledge (jñāna) is the result of the purity of mind attained by the performance of actions unattached. Neither abstaining from action nor be renunciation of actions leads to action-lessness (naiṣkarmya) and perfection respectively (III-4). Because the acts of worship performed in this life or previous birth conduce to the nullification of sins committed and cause purity of mind (sattvaantaḥ-karṇa) which in turn causes knowledge through the path of devotion. Since performance of action is a means of attaining freedom from activity, there is no freedom from activity by abstaining from action. Even in ordinary paralance action is superior to inaction. It is also wrong to suppose that actions lead to bondage and one should abstain from actions because it is the action that sets wheel of the world going. Actions are to be performed without attachment for the sake of God and self-purification of the mind (sattva-suddhi).

There is a distinction between an ignorant man's attitude towards action and that of wise man's. An ignorant man believes that he shoulp do the action and enjoy its result. However a wise man on the contrary thinks that actions are brought in all cases by the energies of Nature. It is by virtue of the guṇas or the modifications of the nature sattva (goodness), rajas (activity), tamas (darkness) manifesting themselves as the body and the sense all our actions conducive to temporal and spiritual ends are done, and an ignorant man falsely thinks that he is the doer. However wise man does not think so, for he identifies himself with the soul.

Modern understanding of Karma as voluntary action. The word karma as action implies intentions of an agent, because karmas are not blindly performed by the agents whether they are wise or ignorant. In other words karma as an intentional action consists of agent's willing in one way or the other, thus they are not unintentional. Thus karma is not involuntary action. Even though intentionality is a necessary component of karma, for a given karma there might be different reasons. A worldly man performs an act a for selfish reason say enjoyment of its fruits as the consequence, however spiritual man (jñāni) would perform for spiritual reasons say purification of internal organ (satva-s'uddhi). Thus karmas are rational actions, for they are to be performed for agent's reasons, and they are also volitional acts. There are general causes of an act right or wrong. Further additional factors like conformity with śāstra etc. qualify a given karma as good karma. Consequently an act *a* is morally right if and only if it is generated in human body or agent through the functioning of mind and sense-organs and it is performed in accordance with śāstras (scriptures). However there is a finer distinction regarding the performancc of a permissible act due to change of intentionality, because what sort of work is performed depends upon the nature of intentionality. If an act *a* (karma) is a performed by ignorant man with the intention of selfish enjoyment then that act is spiritually inferior compared to the same act performed by another agent say a wise man with the intention of self-purification devoid of sensuous utility. Thus two types of intentionality namely utilitarian i.e. sensuous and categorical or spiritual. There seems to be a negative relationship between sensuous intentionality and spiritual intentionality in the sense that they are incompatable. Eventhough sensuous intentions are indispensable in ordinary affairs, they are to be refined or replaced by spiritual intentionality. Sensuous intentionality causes psychological barriers for agent's spiritual development by way of causing perpetual stress and strain at psychic level which in turn affect the entire personality. The criterion of spiritual intentionality is structured in the natuee of self-knowledge i.e. the real understanding of the I by way of removing egoism and super imposition of material factors on the self. Spiritual intentionality implies self-knowledge, consequently actions with spiritual intentions cause spiritual development.

Moral or Spiritual Evaluation of Action (*Karma*) :

Traditionally karmas have been classified into four categories (i) nitya, (ii) naimittika, (iii) kāmya and (iv) pratisiddha. (i) Nitya karmas as obligatory actions are to be performed every day as per vedic injunctions. Permitted acts like agnihotra is a typical nitya karma; often fruits of obligatory actions are not mentioned. Such acts being obligatory imply moral necessity on an agent that he it ought to be performed and its non-performance will entail bad results. Thus there is the necessity of its performance to maintain normal religious life. Śaṅkara seems to be critical about such acts (ii) naimittika karmas as occasional actions are religious acts to be performed on special occasions For example the full moon, and new moon sacrifices are to be performed only on special occasions but not daily. (iii) Kāmya karmas as special type of actions are to be performed in order to achieve specific ends or the fulfilment of desires like the birth of son etc. (iv) Pratisiddha karmas are prohibited actions; their absence say non-performance or obstaining from such actions is conducive to moral life, otherwise they would yield undesirable consequences as hindrances to religi- ous life. Thus they are to be avoided. According to the Pūrvamīmāṃsā, in order to attain the highest end of man i e. paramapuruśārtha it issues the injunctions i.e. imperatives that *do* nitya karmas in order to avoid bad consequences, and also do not do also pratiśiddha karma to avoid bad consequences.

However in the background of jñāna-mārga, Śaṅkara's approach to above types of action is revolutionary. Since ritualistic actions yield fruits in the form of enjoyment, they are inadequate for spiritual progress. However that does not mean that Śaṇkara is against any role played by karma, he recognizes the necessity of karma for the beginners in spiritual life. Even though karmas are necessary at a primary level, Śaṇkara has given a caution that mere karmas lead to bondage but not spiritual freedom. In this context Sri Ātmānanda Swami thinks that the word karma has more than one sense : it means rituals and the like and it means also 'activity' in general. The Swamiji points out a great confusion in the use of the words 'karma' in the teachings of Śaṅkara, if karma means actions in general but not in its special sense as nitya, naimityika karmas i.e. to say ritualistic karmas. Thus it is wrong to say that Śaṇkara has advocated cessation of all activities in general. However he condemns pravritti-karma alone, the activities leading the mind away from the ātman which is against one's naturalistic spiritual inclination. Śaṅkara's own life is a better example for the refutation of passivity, his life was full of intense activities. By way of advocating nivritti mārga he instructs us for ceaselesss effort (yatna) to check the mental modifications in order to turn it towards Ātman. There is also a technique of transforming theory of ordinary karmas into yoga of karmas i e. karma-yoga so that karmas would accelarate spiritual progress. That is to say that karmas instead of causing bondage they lead to freedom. Since karma originates in desire (kāma), it is desire that binds man but not action (karma) itself. If the desire for fruit is given up then the mind retains its original state of equanimity. Accordingly supreme duty is action without desire. However action without desire does not mean unmotivated or unintentional acts but acting with spiritual intentions by way of submission to God. The theory of action in Gita and Śaṇkara's thought does not imply utilitarianism. Because utilitarianism provides a criterion of morality in terms of the consequences of actions leading to pleasure or absence of pleasure. Accordingly an act *a* is morally right if and only if its performance gives rise to greater utility or happiness than its alternative, otherwise that act would be wrong. Thus according to utilitarian criterion of motality pleasure i.e. happiness is an important factor in a moral situation. Utilitarian criterion of morality implies desires for action and fulfilment of desires. Since there is no refined distinction regarding the human pleasures it would be wrong to treat utilitarian critarion for spiritual progress. From spiritual point of view actions loaded with base or lower desires lack any spiritual force, because of consumption of psychic energy for the satisfaction of base or ignoble desires. Thus there is the need of preservation of psychic energy by performing actions for higher spiritual ends However Kant's criterion of morality as expressed in his categorical imparative seems to be very closure to the theory of niṣkāma karma. The categorical imperative as a criterion of morality implies the universalizability of moral rules. Accordingly an agent while performing a given act must be able to will that the maxim of his action should be universal law and the agent follows the rule autonomously. According to this criterion of morality actions should be performed in the sense of duty devoid of any selfish desires otherwise actions performed with any selfih desire or inclination is considered to be wrong act. Human beings are asked to perform their acts only as duty and moral rule to be observed autonomously without any external compulsion. Like niṣkāma-karma, categorical insperative aims at spiritual goal of performing one's duty in order to have moral satisfaction. And both the theories aim at the observance of moral codes or rules. Under similar conditions human beings act in similar ways. Moral responsibilily and moral awareness are important aspects of moral actions, unconditional moral behaviour would bring real moral satisfaction. There is an appreciation of spiritual element in human being by way of following the method of actions without considering utilitarian values. However niṣkāma-karma and categorical imperative seem to provide higher order of spiritual satisfaction.

Meaning of karma : Karma is act or deed but karma as divine service leds to the highest. Even though the word 'karma' literally means 'which is done' 'a deed' or 'action', it signifies spiritual action also. Prof. Hiriyanna observe that a characteristic of all voluntary deeds is that they are preceded by a desire for something which is described as their motive of phala. Accordingly action implies purification of heart which is a necessary condition of self-realization. Bhagavadgīta also teaches the golden mean or the middle path between the pravrtti and nivrtti i.e. the harmoney between renunciation in action and that of renunciation of action. It is possible for a realized man to continue to work for the welfare of the world. For an ordinary man karmamārga is the path of right through which he can reach the goal of perfection. It is through work human beings are brought into relation in the world. Regarding the exact import of karma-yoga it is said that it does not support an ascetic ethics because it reinterprets the Buddhist theory of inaction in a positive way. Accordingly true inaction is action without selfish hope or reward. Niṣkāmatā or disinterestedneess for spiritual benefit is the law of morality. The divine desire of righteousness is permitted. Prof. Radhakrishnan observes : "Whatever we do has to be done not in subjection to an external law, but in obedience to the inner determination of the Soul's freedom". He implies that this is the highest kind of action. According to Aristotle : "He is the best who acts on his own convictions, while he is second best in obedience to the councel of others". Thus good karma or work has to be done in purity of motive so that it purifies the mind in order to acquire spitual wisdom.

In Advaita ethics the law of karma is assumed because individuality is due to karma. An individual as a working machinary is inclined to produce actions having the consequences of pleasure and pain. Prof. Radhakrishnan (635) observes : "moral life is unremitting active energising which is never exhausted". Morality is a stepping stone and not stopping-place. All acts done with an expectation of reward yield their fruits in accordance with the law of karma, while those done with no selfish interest, in the spirit of dedication to God, purify the mind". However individual (jīva) are not like pupets in the hands of the law of karma. Because individual is responsible for his acts and God is only the medium of assistance and God does not compel anybody to do any act. Thus every individual is free to overcome and check his own tendencies by the strength of will.

If Brahman alone exists and the world of plurality is a shadow then there is no real distinction between good and evil. That is to say that if the life is unreal then moral distinctions are not valid if the life is real then they are, valid. This objection is invalid because the world is not treated as mere illusion there is practical reality (vyavahārika satta) in it. Consequently for all practical purposes the world is real and moral values are valid as they lead to the supreme end. In the world love, wisdom asceticism help to attain higher spiritual goals. The world has the real basis of Brahman and not even the mirage can exist without a basis. Eventhough the world is not the essential truth of Brahman it has its phenomenal truth characterised by finite experiences of the world. Śaṅkara urges that mokṣa does not mean the disappearance of the world, it is change of perspective in terms of real spiritual vision or outlook.

It might be objected that on the idea of the metaphpsical identity of the individual self and the absolute there is also no necessity of ethics; every where there is Brahman and there is no need to persue moral goals. This objection is also invalid because it rests upon a confusion between eternal and the temporal reality and the existence Ethical distinctions cannot be invalidated on the basis of the metaphysical one-ness of Brahman. As in the practical world certain things are avoided others desired, so even though all things are ultimately Brahman there are certain things to be avoided and others to be desired. Import of the mahāvākya "aham brahmāsmi" ("I am Brahman") is that the individual attains identity with the reality when the false imposition is removed. There is a constant struggle within the individual self on account of real nature of the self having the condition of intlgrity and the present state of corruption due to ignorance. There is the meaning for struggle with imperfection in order to realize the spiritual goal of self-realization.

Advaita ethics is based on rational fundations of jñāna-yoga. According to it avidya or non-descrimiation is the cause of bondage. Samyagjñāna i.e spiritual insight of oneness leads to freedom. The notion of avidyakāma-karma implies that the whole attitude of individualistic action is rooted in a confusion between the real and the unreal. The discipline of moral life leads to the suppression of selfish activity and the development of true desire like self-realization. Thus moral life is related to the spiritual goal of self-realization (ātma-jñāna).

BIBLIOGRAPHY

1 Atmananda Sawami (1960) : *Sri Sankara's Teachings in his own words.* Bharatiya-Vidya Bhavan, Bombay.

2 Mahadeva Sastri A (1972) : *The Bhagavad-gita* with the commentary of Sri Sankaracarya, (Translation from Sanskrit into English). V.R. Sastri and Sons, Madras.

3. Krishna-Warrier, A.G. (1983) : *Srimad Bhagavad-Gita* Bhasya of Sri Sankaracarya (Translation) Sri Ramakrishna math, Madras.

4. Kant, I. : *Ground work of Metaphysics of morals.*

5. Feldman, F. (1978) : *Introductory Ethics.* Prentics Hall, India.

BIBLIOGRAPHY

1. Annambhatta : (1780) : *Tarka-Samgraha and Dīpikā*, Verse 17. Bhandarkar Oriental Research Institute, Poona.
2. Anscombe, G.E.M. (1975) : *Intention.* Basil Blackwell, Oxford.
3. Aristotle (1949) : *Ethica Nichomachean* in the Works of Aristototle, Vol. IX, Translated by W.D. Ross, Oxford University Press, London.
4. Aune, B. (1972) : '*Intention*' in *Encyclopeadia of Philosophy*, Edited by P. Edwards, Vol. IV, pp. 198-200. Collier MacMillan London.
5. Aune, B. (1972) : '*Thinking*' in *Encyclopeadia of Philosophy* Edited by P. Edwards, Vol. VIII, pp. 102-3 Collier Macmillan, London.
6. Atmananda Swami (1960) : *Sri Śaṅkara's Teachings in his own words.* Bharatiya Vidya Bhavan, Bombay.
7. Austin, J.L. (1961) : 'Ifs and Cans' in *Philosophical Papers*, pp. 153-80. The Clarendon Press, Oxford.
8. Ayer, A.J. (1986) : *Freedom and Morality*, Clarendon Press, Oxford.
9. Brandt, R. (1989) : 'Practical Rationality' in *Philosophy and Phenomenological Research*, Vol. L. No. 1, pp. 125-30, Brown University.
10. Bhattacharya, J.V. (1978, Tr): *Nyāya Mañjarī of Jayanta Bhaṭṭa*, Motilal Banarasidass, Delhi.
11. Copi, I.M. (1973) : *Symbolic Logic.* MacMillan Co., New York.
12. Danto, A.C. (1973) : *Analytical Philosophy of Action.* Cambridge University Press.

13. Davidson, D. (1985) : *Essays on Actions and Events*, Clarendon Press, Oxford.

14. Feldman, F. (1978) : *Introductory Ethics*, Prentice Hall, India.

15. Grayling, A C. (1982) : *An Introduction to Philosophical* Logic, The Harvester Press, Sussex.

16. Hempel, C.G. (1965) : *Aspects of Scientific Explanation*, Collier Macmillan, Ltd., London.

17. Hudson, W.D. (1970) : *Modern Moral Philosophy*, *Macmillan* and Co., London.

18. Kalish, D.R., Montague and Garyman, (1980) : *Logic : Techniques of Formal Reasoning*, Jovanovich, Inc., N.Y. London

19 Kant I : *Ground work of Metaphysics of morals.*

20. Kripke S (1984): *Naming and Necessity*, Basil Blackwell, Oxford.

21. Krishna-Warrier, A.G. (1983) : *Srimad Bhagavad-Gita Bhosya of Sri Sankaracharya* (Translation) Sri Ramakrishna Math, Madras.

22. Jha, Ganganatha (Tr.) : *Sloka-Vartika of Kumarila*, Indian Books Centre, Delhi

23. Jha, V.N. (1986) : *The Logic of Intermediate Causal Link*, Indian Books Centre, Delhi.

24. Linksy, L. (1977) : *Names and Descriptions*, Chicago University Press.

25. Madhavananda S. (1977 : *Bhasha-Parichheda B.P.) with Siddhanta-Muktavali* (Ed, & Tr.) Advaita Ashram, Calcutta.

26. Mahadeva Sastri A (1972) : *The Bhagavad-gita with the commentary of Sri Sankaracharya*, (Tr.) V.R. Sastri and Sons, Madras.

27. Malcolm, N. (1989) : '*Wittgenstein on Language and Rules*' *in Philosophy*, Vol. 64, No. 247, pp. 5-28, R.I;P. London.

28. Moore, G.E. (1959) : *Principia Ethica*, Cambridge, University Press, Cambridge.

29. Putnam, H. (1975) : *Mind, Language and Reality*, Vol. 2, Cambridge University, Press, Cambridge.

30. Quine, W.V.O. 1972 : *Methods of Logic*, Halt Rinehart, New York.

31. Quinn, W.S. (1989) : '*Actions, Intentions and Consequences*' in The Philosophical Review, Vol. 'XC VIII, No. 3, pp. 287-312, Cornell University.

32. Reichenbach, H. (1947) : *Elements of Symbolic Logic*, MacMillan Co., New York.

33. Salmon, N.U. (1982) : *Reference and Essence*, Basil Blackwell, Oxford.

34. Strawson, P.F. (1974) : *Freedom and Resentment*, Methuen and Co., London.

35. Visvanatha (1700) : *Bhasha Parichheda with Siddhanta-Muktavali*, Choukamba Sanskrit Series, Varanasi

36. Wittgedstein, L. (1953) : *Philosophical Investigations*, Translated by G.E.M. Anscombe, Basil Blackwell Oxford.

37. Whitehead, A.N. and Russel B. (1950) *Principia Mathematica* (Vol. 1), Cambridge.

38. Woozley A.D. (1967) : *Theory of Knowledge*, Hutchinson, London.

INDEX OF WORDS